Praise for 7

MW00424927

Wow, wow, wow. I absolutely LOVE
any individual looking to shift from
life. The stories are captivating and the principles that Devin shares are pure trutn.
This book has inspired me to re-examen the values in my own life and helped me
to recognize many areas of improvement.

Noelle Pikus Pace, World Champion and Olympic Medalist

I've known Devin for many years and can attest to his passion for making a positive
difference in the lives of those around him. This innovative work offers a fresh take
on the importance of identifying and connecting personal values to individual
happiness and success.

Taylor R. Randall, President, University of Utah

Devin's message of the power of doing small and simple things resonates with me.
During my football career and now as a business executive and sports analyst,
I've seen time and time again in business, sports, and at home how small, focused
efforts can lift people to greater heights and successes. Devin does a great job of
presenting time-tested ideas in a new and easily attainable way. Enjoy the journey
through the pages of this inspiring book!

Steve Young, NFL Hall of Fame Quarterback

Devin's new book is a revelation, filled with fresh insights and inspiring stories.
Who thought you could quantify VALUES? Devin did. This book will transform
and elevate your thinking on Values (what Devin calls Priority Values) - the moral
values most important to us today. Devin's life is the embodiment of his book -
you can feel his authenticity and credibility in the pages of his book.

**David M. R. Covey, Bestselling author of *Trap Tales: Outsmarting the 7
Hidden Obstacles to Success and CEO of SMCOVEY***

Our organization and family regard our core values of hard work, integrity, service,
and stewardship as fundamental to everything we do – they are the foundation of
who we are. Devin Durrant's book *The Values Delta*, helps readers reflect, evaluate,
and practice values to become the best version of themselves. Durrant's shared
stories and easy-to-use tools are applicable in our personal and professional lives.
This book is a valuable resource for building a solid foundation based on ethics
and values.

Gail Miller, Founder and Owner of the Larry H. Miller Company

The Values Delta: A Small & Simple Way To Make a Positive Difference In Your Personal & Professional Life is a must read. Values are something that are important to me, and by reading this book it only enhances my relationships with my family, friends, and work colleagues. The Values Delta Report Card and the four delta steps will help you understand your values and then use them to impact the people in your lives and yourself in a positive way. I love how this book is sending a positive message to everyone while increasing your chances of success!

Jimmer Fredette, Professional Athlete/Entrepreneur

This wonderful book shows how vitally important and impactful it is to first identify and then live by your values. This process is both freeing and empowering. Filled with terrific examples and authentic stories, Devin shows how embracing your true priorities can brighten your future and expand your possibilities--both personally and professionally. And Devin's a tremendous model of what he teaches.

Stephen M. R. Covey, The New York Times and #1 Wall Street Journal bestselling author of *The Speed of Trust* and *Trust & Inspire*

The Values Delta can lead to meaningful change in your life! Devin introduces a quantitative approach to identifying and developing our best qualities and applying that focus to the people and things of greatest significance to us. Take Devin's challenge and get to know yourself better!

Greg Wrubell, "Voice of the Cougars" BYU radio play-by-play broadcaster

Devin's book *The Values Delta* really hit home the importance of listing and recognizing your values and what you stand for. From the minute I started to read, I could not stop or put this book down. His book made a huge positive difference in my personal life as well as my professional life! This is my best day so far! I do the small and simple things that make a powerful difference. Devin, "Thanks for the cab ride!"

Ed Terris, Vice President Sales, KT Tape

Devin's book is extremely timely as we all reevaluate our lives and where we go from here. Everyone needs to add new and more value to our existing and surviving values to help give direction and faith in our new lives that will emerge. I will treasure and value this book as a key source for needed inspiration and direction. Devin is a prime example for us all to follow in becoming a better father and parent, friend, trusted business associate, leader and boss.

Phil Hoopes, Sr. Founder, Hoopes Vision

In *The Values Delta*, my longtime friend and inspirational mentor Devin Durrant, doesn't just teach what he knows – he teaches what he lives, who he is, what he's done – offering the solution to the most critical dilemma of our day: Most people hate their jobs, only look forward to Friday instead of Monday, thinking they are paid by the hour, when, we are all paid for the value we bring to that hour. As a 'behavioral bible,' *The Values Delta* illuminates that the way we make ourselves more valuable is to embrace a set of Core Values, or Priority Values, as Devin calls them. Because the purpose of a leader is to grow more leaders who believe what you believe, not generate more followers, Devin explains that when we get ourselves and everybody in our families, businesses, sports teams, and schools to live by the Highest Values and follow the Daily Delta Plan - significant relationships, extreme profitability, character-based education, and winning take care of themselves! A must read if you're serious about up-leveling who you really are!

Dan Clark, Hall of Fame Speaker and New York Times Bestselling Author of The Art of Significance

Devin has been a great source of spiritual strength and information to me for many years. If you are looking for ways to feel more joy in your life, read this great book. You will find that a positive delta will be the outcome of pondering from these pages!

Chad Lewis, Former Philadelphia Eagles 3-Time Pro Bowl Selection at Tight End

Devin Durrant has identified an elegantly simple approach to help individuals, families, and organizations assess, prioritize, and identify the key values that are driving their behaviors. I recommend you read his book and apply his principles and methodology!

Lon E. Henderson, CEO, Ampelis LLC

If you know Devin then you know he loves life. He is optimistic, kind, hard-working and he cares deeply for others. Devin lives life purposefully. I have often wondered "What's his secret?" In *The Values Delta*, he outlines a simple pattern that, if followed, can harness your God-given talents and develop your desired talents to make you a better person and uplift those around you. The stories and methods shared here succinctly convey the principles and processes to achieve outcomes that are reachable by anyone willing to take a little time to achieve a meaningful result as a short-term effort or a long-term way of living. It's an extremely enjoyable and motivational read.

Kimball E. Hodges, Founder and COO, Wasatch Energy Management, LLC

As a business leader and a dad, this book has had a tremendous practical effect on how I conduct myself with others. Devin's two questions allowed me to define myself through a set of values! Once I had defined "me", the Values Delta Report Card was a powerful tool for honestly measuring progress toward a better me.

David Mink, CEO, Avalaunch Media

The Values Delta took me on a journey of introspection of where I place the most value in my own life; not only by providing helpful tools and insights, but through the authors own vulnerabilities and personal experiences. As a small business owner I found this simple, yet impactful invitation to be transformational in how I intend to interact, motivate, and lead my team going forward. A brilliant personal growth playbook!

Kym Nelson, SealSource International, LLC, President and Founder

Living in a world of turmoil can be exhausting at times. It can feel as if the world is spinning out of control. The principles in *The Values Delta* outline a simple path for companies and individuals to regain a sense of control over the most meaningful aspects of our lives. I particularly appreciated the report cards because they are an easy tool to aid in positive change and stability for me and my business.

Wright J. Thurston Sr., Entrepreneur and Professional Speaker

Devin has done it again. Growing up, Devin inspired me to be a better basketball player. In college, he mentored and helped me start my real estate investing career. And now through his book, *The Values Delta*, Devin has once again inspired me to identify my key values and then focus on simple ways that I can improve them. This is a valuable exercise for individuals and companies. I enjoyed and highly recommend *The Values Delta* to everyone!

Jacob Hawkins, Chief Marketing, Digital and Omni Officer at Forever 21

If you desire to more closely align your character with your values—for yourself, your family, or your company—and you're looking for uncomplicated and effective motivation to do just that, this book is for you. Devin leads you through his simple strategy in the early pages of the book, then gives you case studies and insight to inspire meaningful change. Engaging, humorous, and authentic. Applicable to people of all ages and circumstances who want to raise their game to a higher level.

Camille Fronk Olson, Author and Teacher

The Values Delta has given me an optimistic approach to prioritizing my values, both personally and professionally. With this book, you're able to re-examine your morals and values through a new lens, giving you an improved path forward in which to make a 'delta' in life – positively affecting your family and colleagues.

Lee Johnson, 18-year NFL career as a punter

THE VALUES DELTA

Dedicated to my beloved 16 grandchildren (and counting). May each of you always strive to make the world a better place by living true to your Priority Values.

COUGAR HILL PUBLISHING
2000 North Canyon Road
Provo, UT 84604

ISBN: 978-1-7374578-0-0 (print)
ISBN: 978-1-7374578-1-7 (ebook)
Ordering Information:
Special discounts are available on quantity purchases by corporations, associations, and
others. For details, go to thevaluesdelta.com.

Contents

THE VALUES DELTA

A
Small
& Simple
Way To

Make
A Positive
Difference

In Your Personal &
Professional Life

Devin Durrant

PART ONE

Getting to Know Yourself

What are your values? I'm guessing it may have been a while since you last gave this question some thought. Take a minute or two and think about your answer.

If you're struggling to identify your most important values, don't feel bad. You're not alone. Before I delved deeply into contemplating how our values impact so many aspects of our lives, I didn't give the listing of my values much importance either.

Next, think about who or what you most value in your life. That could include your spouse, your children, your business or job, your parents, your friends, your neighbors…as well as yourself.

As you read this book, you will see the significance of the "Values Delta" and how it impacts what you most treasure in your life.

Highest Highs and Lowest Lows

As we embark on this journey together, allow me to share several personal highest highs as well as lowest lows. I start with some highest highs from a "few" years back in junior high school. As a 7th grader I was elected president of my entire school (7th through 9th grade). I was then re-elected president for both my 8th and 9th grade years. Those were fun times for a young boy.

As a senior in high school, my Provo High Bulldogs went undefeated, and we won the state championship in basketball. I was named to the McDonald's All-American team. A few weeks later, I won the Derby Classic one-on-one competition, held in Louisville, Kentucky. The competitors were the participants in the Derby Classic—an invitation-only gathering featuring the best high school players in the country. That night I led my team, the United States All-Stars, to victory over the Kentucky-Indiana All-Stars and was selected as the Most Valuable Player of the game. As a result of these successes, a veteran sportswriter referred to me as the best high school basketball player in America.[1]

In college, my Brigham Young University Cougars won our league two out of four years. I led the nation in scoring for most of my senior year and was a consensus All-American. I was then chosen with the 25th pick of the 1984 NBA draft—the strongest draft class ever—featuring Hakeem Olajuwon, Charles Barkley, John Stockton, and Michael Jordan to name a few. Speaking of highs and lows and Michael Jordan, I am one of the few people who can say I dunked on Michael (at the Olympic Trials—1984) and was dunked on by Michael (Chicago Bulls vs. Indiana Pacers—1985).

On the lowest lows side athletically, my team lost twice (sophomore and junior year) in the semifinals of the state championship. In college, we got knocked out of the NCAA tournament in the first or second round three times. I was cut from two NBA teams. All these moments brought feelings of failure and disappointment.

In the business world, I have reaped some amazing highest highs rewards. I had the privilege of playing a key role in the largest software application rollout in history, up to that time. I have also been involved in real estate transactions that have netted my companies millions of dollars.

On the lowest lows side in business, I have performed miserably in front of hundreds of people during a software competition—very embarrassing. I have also suffered through business collapses and lost well over a million dollars in various failed investments. On some days, I have felt super smart. On other days, I have felt just the opposite. Can you relate?

On the high side, I have been extremely blessed with cherished family and friends who have helped me experience some of life's

---

1   Linda Hamilton, *Deseret News*, May 9, 1978.

greatest joys. Sadly, on the low side, I have experienced the heartache of serious physical and mental illness in family and friends, and the deep sorrow of losing loved ones. I have also tasted the bitterness of relationships gone sour.

I have enjoyed some great jobs, and I have been jobless. I have lived in spacious, well-furnished homes, and I have lived in small one-bedroom apartments with boxes as furniture.

Looking back, I can see how my values motivated and helped me reach the highest of highs. They also sustained, guided, and comforted me through the lowest of lows. Your values can do that for you too. They can also help you make a positive difference in a variety of small and simple ways. That is the focus of this book.

Delta

The first four letters of the Greek alphabet are alpha, beta, gamma, and delta. We're focusing on delta. The uppercase symbol for delta is Δ and its numeric value is 4. There are various dictionary definitions for the term delta. Merriam-Webster defines it as "an increment of a variable,"[2] but I am going to use a less technical definition: a difference or a change in something.

The word delta commonly means the difference between two numbers. For example, the delta between the numbers 10 and 3 is 7. However, my purpose with this book is to help you make a positive delta—difference or change—in your life and in the lives of those close to you. These principles and ideas also apply to your company, organization, association, or institution.

---

2   "Delta," Merriam-Webster, accessed March 11, 2021, https://www.merriam-webster.com/dictionary/delta.

A delta can be either positive or negative. Throughout this book, in order to reduce the overuse of the term "positive" when I use the terms "delta," "difference," and "change," I will always use them in the positive sense, unless I state otherwise.

Why?

As mentioned previously, I played basketball at BYU, and went on to play professional basketball for the Indiana Pacers and briefly for the Phoenix Suns when I was in my 20s. I then enjoyed a long career in business after I left professional sports, including being a marketing director at WordPerfect Corporation during my 30s and owning my own real estate investment firm during my 40s and beyond.

My adult life has also been enriched with many opportunities to serve and work alongside thousands of college-aged men and women in various settings. I thank each of them for keeping me young at heart (even when the calendar says differently) and for inspiring me by being loyal to their values!

In addition, I have had the fortunate opportunity to speak to a wide variety of audiences around the world. I love interacting with people from different backgrounds. My presentations have addressed interests ranging from athletics to education, and from investments to parenting. My audiences have included faith-based groups and business-centric groups. As a side note, I think I may have given more values-based talks to more people in more countries than any ex-professional athlete ever. Could we add that tidbit to the next edition of Trivial Pursuit? Seriously, as you will soon see, I have strong feelings about the significance of moral values and their influence on the people and things that are most important in our lives.

My purpose in my talks and in this book is to draw renewed attention to your values and the difference they make on the people and things you most value in your personal and professional life. That's my why.

My Father

As a young boy, I enjoyed working at the side of my father, George Durrant. I particularly enjoyed helping him with outdoor projects around our house. I was energized when he said to me, "Devin, having you help me is like having a man's help." I was young and knew my contribution wasn't making much of a difference, but my father's words inspired me. As the years passed and I was able to physically offer my father more help, I received the priceless treasure of confidence. My father instilled in me the desire to give my best effort. His words and example made the values of work and confidence an integral part of who I am today. Over my lifetime, I have tried to do for my children and others what my father did for me—create delta with the values of work and confidence, in addition to other moral values.

In the United States, we often refer to "our values" in a general sense, but we rarely talk about specific values and if and how they make a *difference*. It feels good to talk about "our values," but we are missing out on the true benefits of focusing on what we define as "our values" and how they impact what we truly value, be it our loved ones, our profession, our passion, and, maybe most important of all, ourselves.

Priority Values

One of my objectives in writing this book is to invite conversations about what we most value in our lives and how a focus on our Priority Values (similar to core values) impacts those precious people and things that we most value, in small and large ways. For clarity, our Priority Values are simply the moral values that are most important to us today—the values that have the highest priority in our lives. These values can be expressed with words you would use to describe the most important traits you or your organization possess.

As you read and ponder the values chapters that follow in Part Two, you will learn more regarding conversations about values. Also, I will outline the Priority Values that have served me well in my personal and professional life. As you engage in these conversations and reflect on your own personal and organizational values and their significance, I hope to clarify how you can do these two things more effectively:

1. Understand what your Priority Values are and how they can help you make a positive difference with what you value most.

2. Help instill moral values in others that help them create delta and add meaning and strength to what they value.

Judgment

Please understand this book is not about me or anyone else making judgments about you and your values. The only judgments made about you will be made by you, which I will encourage. My goal is to provide an introspective experience that provides you a path to greater hope, success, and satisfaction in your life regardless of your gender, race, political views, religious affiliation, or any other aspect of your life that might be considered divisive or open to judgment. I believe that stated objective can be achieved through a small and simple focus on positive values in your personal life and/or in your profession.

A quote by author and historian W. L. Sheldon from an essay published in 1897 has left an impression on me: "There is nothing noble in being superior to your fellow men. True nobility lies in being superior to your former self."[3]

---

3   W. L. Sheldon, "What to Believe: An Ethical Creed," in *Ethical Addresses* (Philadelphia: American Ethical Union, 1895–1914), 61.

What an optimal way to look at delta! I have come to see and understand that the best way to create delta in all the things I value is to add to my Priority Values. May you become superior to your former self as you read and apply the content in the chapters ahead.

I offer this book as my humble attempt to do good in the world and lift my readers and those they interact with to a better place in their lives, one value at a time.

The Flight

Let's start to understand delta creation more clearly with two stories about my interactions with a woman I'll call Michelle, and later, with a man I'll call Rick. The stories didn't happen exactly as I tell them. They are, however, compilations of bits and pieces from a number of conversations and experiences I have had and hope to have, combined into two accounts, to lay a foundation on which we can build. Here we go with the first story.

Several years ago, my wife, Julie, and I drove to the airport, anticipating four quiet hours on an airplane as we flew from Los Angeles to Chicago. Julie purchased a thick paperback she wanted to read—she loves to read, and a long flight promised to be an opportunity to immerse herself in an interesting book. Unlike Julie, I dreaded curling my six foot seven inch frame into a small airplane seat for several hours, but my laptop in my travel bag would offer a chance to focus on a neglected task that needed to be completed. We looked forward to the solitude, a relaxing meal, and a break from our usual routines. We did not plan on Michelle, the woman across the aisle. We soon learned that she was not only gregarious and friendly, but full of curiosity and questions that started as soon as I opened my laptop.

"So, what are you working on?" Michelle asked.

Safe in her window seat, Julie smiled as she ducked her head further into her book. I looked up from my laptop, finally sensing the question was directed toward me.

"Oh, I'm sorry. I didn't realize you were talking to me. I'm writing a book," I said.

Michelle grinned as she glanced at my screen.

"Does anyone really read anymore, beyond their social media updates? Are you trying to fix that with the next great American novel?" she queried.

I chuckled uneasily. She then asked, "What business are you in?"

I thought for a moment, then said, "I am in the business of creating delta. In other words, I work to make a positive difference in value where I can."

I could tell Michelle hadn't any idea of what I meant, so I added, "I am a real estate investor. I add value to properties by solving their problems. For example, if I buy an apartment complex, I work to create an increase in value by operating the property more efficiently. Once I feel that has happened, I begin to consider selling the property for a profit. But more important than adding monetary value to property, I am writing this book to help people create delta in all areas of their lives—in their homes, at the workplace, and in their social groups. But mostly, I want to help them add value by creating a positive difference in themselves by helping them focus on their personal values."

"Your book is going to change the world then?" she asked with a smile.

"Maybe not the world," I responded. "But I hope it will change at least one person or one organization for the better." I continued, "My book is about helping individuals, families, and other groups of people with a common interest to discover how to create delta in the people and things they truly value by enhancing and magnifying their current set of Priority Values."

Sensing I had lost her, I backed up. "I'm sorry," I said. "I never asked your name."

"Michelle," she said, simultaneously holding out her hand.

I shook her hand adding, "It's very nice to meet you, Michelle. This is my wife, Julie." Julie lowered her book and nodded politely. "And my name is Devin Durrant."

"Kevin Durant, the famous basketball player?" she asked incredulously, which prompted a quick laugh from Julie.

"No, Devin Durrant," I clarified, with emphasis on the "D" in Devin. "But I am a big Kevin Durant fan. I love his game."

> "Values are like fingerprints. Nobody's are the same, but you leave 'em all over everything you do."
> – Attributed to Elvis Presley

"Ah!" she said. "With your height, I *thought* maybe you spent a lot of time playing basketball."

Julie couldn't resist jumping in, and added, "When he was a college senior, after we married, he was the leading scorer in the country and was a consensus All-American. He later played in the NBA in the Michael Jordan, Charles Barkley, and Patrick Ewing era." She smiled and then pretended to concentrate again on her book (I adore my "publicist" wife).

Michelle redirected the conversation back to my writing. She asked, "But now you create delta? That's your profession?"

"Yes, I try to!" I said. "When my career path turned away from basketball, I found that the values of hard work, self-confidence, and toughness—values that allowed me to be successful as an athlete— also make a difference in real life, away from sports. Now I'm writing a book to help people see the importance of adding to their Priority Values and how that will make a difference in their lives."

"Now, I have a question for you," I said. "What are your Priority Values? She studied my face for a long moment, so I continued. "Let's create a list—your Priority Values—by filling in the blank at the end of this sentence: I would describe myself as a person of _____." Your list can include as many values as you would like, but for our purposes, share with me six to eight values that come to your mind.

I handed Michelle a list of 200+ values to review and consider (see Appendix 1 at the back of the book). After several minutes of reading and reflection, she finally said, "I hope I can honestly say I am a person of thoughtfulness." After pausing to think for a moment, she continued, "And caring and industriousness." She hesitated and then added the values of creativity, wisdom, and generosity.

"Very impressive!" I said. "That is a wonderful way to describe yourself and your values." I told Michelle I appreciated her willingness to be so open with me. I typed her list of Priority Values into my computer. It looked like this:

My Priority Values

1. Thoughtfulness
2. Caring
3. Industriousness
4. Creativity
5. Wisdom
6. Generosity

I then prompted her to think back on her school days. I asked her to recall her college grade point average (GPA) and she said it was 3.8. I was impressed! Then I asked her to go through her list with me and give herself a grade on each of her values using the grading scale that was used back in college (A = 4.0, B = 3.0, C = 2.0, D = 1.0). It was okay, I said, to give herself points between two letter grades as we determine her Value Point Average (VPA).

After a few minutes, we had updated her list with her grades.

My Priority Values

1. Thoughtfulness   3.0
2. Caring   3.5
3. Industriousness   2.5
4. Creativity   3.5
5. Wisdom   3.0
6. Generosity   2.5

After some quick math, we came up with a total of 18.0. That number divided by the six values equaled 3.0. That number, 3.0, represented Michelle's Value Point Average, or VPA.

She frowned at the result. She had been extremely successful in school and had worked hard to earn a high GPA. Her face showed she was already thinking of things she might do to improve her VPA.

"Are you ready to take the next step?" I asked. She replied affirmatively.

"Let's build a second list consisting of four to eight people or things you most value in life. We will do this by filling in the blank in this sentence: My life would be much less meaningful without _____."

Michelle was again willing to go down this path with me, and thought for a few seconds and answered, "My children. My legal career. My friends. And the horse ranch I own and help manage with other family members." I entered these items into my computer. "That's an excellent start," I said and asked for her permission to add her name to the top of the list we were creating. She smiled and agreed.

Michelle's second list looked like this:

Things I Value

1. Myself: Michelle

2. Children

3. Legal career

4. Friends

5. Horse ranch

We then reviewed her two lists together.

My Priority Values

1.	Thoughtfulness	3.0
2.	Caring	3.5
3.	Industriousness	2.5
4.	Creativity	3.5
5.	Wisdom	3.0
6.	Generosity	2.5
	Total:	18.0
VPA (Total/6):		**3.0**

Things I Value

1. Myself: Michelle
2. Children
3. Legal career
4. Friends
5. Horse ranch

As she looked at the two lists, I asked the key question: "In what ways can you make a difference in what you value by adding to your values?" I continued with two more questions. "If you strived to be more *creative*, will that help you advance your legal career? Or if you were more *caring*, would that help you feel better about yourself?" She nodded and said, "I think if I could increase that 3.5 on caring to a 3.75 or a 4.0, my friends would be much happier with me."

She was seeing the vision. Creating delta with the value of caring would certainly increase the bond of her existing—and future—friendships. I liked the direction of our conversation.

Michelle was quiet for a while and asked if she could look at her lists again. I handed her my laptop. After a few minutes she said, "It's too hard. How can I improve in so many areas all at once?" Hesitantly, I explained that it can be hard, but asked her not to let that be the reason for not trying. "I can make it easier," I said, and asked her to try a simple four-step exercise for a week to test out my theory. She agreed.

1. Choose one value from the My Priority Values list that you would like to focus on. Let's call your chosen value the focus value. She chose thoughtfulness. We were headed in a good direction.

2. Choose one item from your Things I Value list that you feel would benefit from a focused effort on thoughtfulness. She chose children and said, "I have three wonderful children—a son and two daughters." She opened her purse and showed me a picture of her family. She took a few minutes to tell me a bit about each child.

3. Do one or more of the following ideas to keep you centered on your objective throughout the week.

    a. Find a picture of something that makes you think of the importance of being thoughtful and post it in a prominent place near a picture of your children.

    b. Find an inspirational quote on thoughtfulness. The Internet makes this easy. Print your quote and put it where you can read it multiple times a day.

    c. Spend a few minutes each day reading/listening to books, articles, podcasts, etc., about thoughtfulness.

    d. Seek opportunities during the week to discuss the importance of the value of thoughtfulness with family, friends, and associates.

Each of these exercises will help you make thoughtfulness a part of your everyday mindset and actions.

4. During the week, do at least one thing to show your thoughtfulness toward your children. I then shared these two sayings with her that have motivated me to act: 1) If you don't do at least one thing, you may end up doing no thing (and you know what that sounds like), and 2) The smallest action blesses more than the greatest intention.

With the first two items completed, she agreed to do the last two and I told her that small and simple efforts sustained over time can produce significant results. I saw in Michelle's eyes that she would make these four small efforts as a starting point to creating delta.

At that point, I pulled out a copy of The Values Delta Report Card, found at the back of this book (Appendix 2), and gave it to her, hoping it would serve as a good reminder of our conversation. I then asked her to send me an email after seven days and report how her children responded, and to please share what impact, if any, the process had on her personally. She agreed.

We began our descent into Chicago, and even though I hadn't made much progress on my neglected task, I enjoyed my conversation with Michelle. She leaned over and said, "Devin, I think what you have shared could not only help me improve myself, but it could also help my horse business." She explained that her passion is horses, and she trains and breeds horses at her ranch with help from her family. She said she felt that if she and her family spent time focusing on values and improving the corporate VPA, their customers would notice, and the financial delta of the net income of the horse business would improve.

Julie closed her book and said, "Michelle, I've been eavesdropping a bit on the conversation between you two. I know how much this subject means to my husband. He has been pondering the topic and teaching it for years in different settings, large and small. It is a simple process that works. I know it will work for you and those you work with if everyone puts in the needed effort. You can make a difference with those things you value by focusing on your values. I've seen it happen for my husband and others as well."

I smiled at Julie. I felt a sense of satisfaction. Michelle now understood more clearly that her values impact all areas of her life. If she focuses on her values individually and collectively the delta will be positive over time, in qualitative and quantitative ways, for herself, her family, her horse business, and her legal career.

Seven days later, right on schedule, I received a wonderful email from Michelle. A portion of the email reads as follows: "I did it! I created positive delta with my children. I worked each day to be more thoughtful with them (kind notes, taking more time to listen, being more sensitive to their needs, etc.) and they noticed a difference! My oldest son even took me aside at the end of the week and said, 'I love you, Mom. You are the perfect mother for me.' It warmed my heart to hear those words from a tough teenage boy."

She concluded her email by telling me she was going to choose a new focus value for the following week and see if she could be a delta maker on a different item on her Things I Value list.

The Lunch

I was pleased to hear of Michelle's positive experience with her family. She saw how a focus on her values would make a big difference in her personal life. But a question still remained. Would a focus on the values of an organization create delta in a large group of people like it might in the life of one individual? I wanted to test it out.

Here is the second story. A good friend of mine, Rick, is the president of a company that is headquartered near my home. I decided to call him and invite him to lunch. I told him I wanted to share some ideas that I believed would help his company. Rick was a well-liked and successful leader. Part of his success came from a willingness to seek new ways to operate more efficiently. Rick said he was open for lunch the following Tuesday. We had a date.

After being seated at the restaurant, Rick and I did some catching up. When a pause in the conversation came, Rick said he was interested to hear what I had for him. I cut to the chase.

"Let me ask you two questions. The first one is, what are your organization's values? Please tell me the top six to eight."

He paused for a minute and then said, "Sure, our values are integrity, customer service, respect, loyalty, and vision. I know there are more, I just can't remember them at the moment."

"That's okay," I said. "I'm going to write these five values down and refer to them as your organization's Priority Values."

Rick then stopped me and said, "I can't remember the rest right now, but they are all written on a large plaque in our main entry."

> "You can't see values, touch them, taste them, or smell them. Yet they are critical, intangible essentials that bring continuity and meaning to life.
>
> And they are every bit as important for organizations as they are for individuals."
> – Harvey Mackay, *You Haven't Hit Your Peak Yet!* p. 184

"We are good for now," I said. "Here's my second question. What does your organization value? What would a list of four to eight items look like? Your answer can include people or things." I then added, "Here's an easy way to complete the list. Finish this sentence. Our organization would be much less meaningful without _____. Let's make the first item on the list your company, DBKC Inc."

Rick thought for about thirty seconds and then said, "Our organization would be much less meaningful without our employees and their families. And we certainly value our customers."

"That's four. Is there anything else you want to include on the list?" I asked.

"Yes, we also value our relationship with the community," Rick said to finish his second list.

I commended Rick for working through these two lists. They looked like this:

Our Priority Values

1. Integrity

2. Customer service

3. Respect

4. Loyalty

5. Vision

Things We Value

1. Our organization: DBKC Inc.

2. Our employees

3. The families of our employees

4. Our customers

5. Our relationship with the communities we serve

I showed Rick the lists and asked him if he wanted to make any additions to his organization's Priority Values. He reached for his phone and checked his organization's website for additional values. He then said, "Add discipline, charity, and punctuality to the values list." I made the changes and the Priority Values list for his organization now looked like this:

Our Priority Values

1. Integrity

2. Customer service

3. Respect

4. Loyalty

5. Vision

6. Discipline

7. Charity

8. Punctuality

Rick then asked me, "So, what's the point of this exercise?"

I responded, "Good question. Let's do one more thing and then I'll tie it all together."

I quickly explained the Value Point Average (VPA) concept to Rick as I had done with Michelle on the plane and asked him to grade each of his organization's Priority Values. He made several comments as he graded each value, some positive and others not so much. Here is the updated Priority Values list with the grades and calculated VPA:

Our Priority Values	Grades
1. Integrity	3.7
2. Customer service	3.0
3. Respect	3.3
4. Loyalty	3.0
5. Vision	3.8
6. Discipline	2.8
7. Charity	3.8
8. Punctuality	2.6
Total:	26
VPA (Total/8):	**3.25**

We took a few minutes to enjoy our food and then got back to the purpose of our meeting.

I showed Rick his two completed lists and his VPA and asked, "What was your GPA in college?" I knew the answer before I asked the question. Nobody was a better student than Rick Spencer. He was also quite competitive.

"4.0," he said.

Then I asked, "Could I show you a small and simple way to increase your organization's VPA?

His eyes widened and he said, "Absolutely!" I knew that the 3.25 VPA had gotten under his skin a bit and he was ready to listen. And I was anxious to share how we might be able to raise that 3.25 to a 3.75 and create a positive delta of .5. And we wouldn't stop there.

I then asked him to think about this next question: "In what ways would a positive delta with one value impact one of the items on your organization's Things We Value list?"

He then said, "Okay, I get it. Let me try to explain it back to you." He continued, "If we focus on our value of respect for one week and how it impacts our customers, positive delta will be created."

"Perfect," I said. I then quickly explained the Value Effect (more on that in a moment) to him and asked, "Who will benefit from the ripples of an emphasis on respect toward your customers?"

Rick responded, "A few answers come to mind: the leaders of our organization, our frontline employees, our customers, and maybe even our vendors and others we interact with throughout the day." He then added, "It will probably also have an uplifting effect in the homes of our employees." Rick then added this last thought. "I'm guessing that if we are more respectful as an organization, there will also be a benefit to the bottom line." I agreed.

I smiled at Rick and proceeded to show him The Values Delta Report Card for organizations (Appendix 3) and explained to him the four steps I wanted him to take with some of his employees over the next eight weeks. These four steps were the same as the ones I outlined for Michelle with some slight modifications for a group instead of an individual.

We paid for our meals, and as Rick and I walked to the door he agreed to give this idea a try in one of his divisions and report back to me down the road. "I will look forward to it," I said as we went our separate ways.

This conversation with Rick took place in February and I didn't hear anything from him until the end of April. I saw his name show up on the caller ID of my phone and I quickly answered. He greeted me cordially, and I smiled when I heard the tone of his voice. He then excitedly told me, "It worked! It worked! Your idea worked."

"Please tell me more," I said. He then went on to explain how he had shared the concept with a few members of his leadership team and asked them to try it out in their divisions. They returned later with various stories of how a focus value had been chosen each week and the impacts the exercise had over time on different items on DBKC's Things We Value list. He also shared how the leaders were able to easily measure delta in some cases and how it was a bit more difficult to measure in other cases, but that for the most part each weekly emphasis on one value had made a positive difference on one or more items on the Things We Value list. One manager even thanked Rick for the idea because he had noticed a financial delta in his department's sales numbers as a result of the exercise.

As you might imagine, Rick's phone call made my day.

Creating Delta: Two Questions

It's your turn now. Consider the following two questions.

Question 1: What Are Your Values?

Your values define who you are. Beyond your haircut or designer clothes, your values are what make you you. As mentioned earlier, your most important values are your Priority Values. My hope is that from this day forward your values take even greater priority in your life.

Carl Rogers, a psychologist who is widely considered to be one of the founding fathers of psychotherapy research and was widely honored for his pioneering work in the field said, "Clarifying your values is the essential first step toward a richer, fuller, more productive life."[4]

Create your list of Priority Values by repeatedly considering and finishing the following statement: "I would describe myself as a

---

4   Harvey Mackay, *You Haven't Hit Your Peak Yet!* (Hoboken: Wiley, 2020), 184.

person of _____." Your list might include "dignity," "kindness," "loyalty," or "humor." You may want to ask someone who knows you well for help with this list. Review the list of values in Appendix 1, then take a few minutes to create your My Priority Values list below. You may also choose to glance at the eight chapter titles in Part Two to stimulate your thinking as you create your list of Priority Values.

My Priority Values	My Grades (1.0–1.4)
1. _____	_____
2. _____	_____
3. _____	_____
4. _____	_____
5. _____	_____
6. _____	_____
7. _____	_____
8. _____	_____
Total:	_____
VPA (Total/8):	_____

Now that you have created your My Priority Values list, give yourself a grade in the column to the right of each of your values using the college grading system (A = 4.0, B = 3.0, C = 2.0, D = 1.0). You may use numeric points between, such as 3.2, for example. Total the numbers, divide it by the number of values you listed, and your answer is your Value Point Average (VPA). Enter it in the space provided.

Question 2: What Do You Value?

The things you value are what give meaning to your life. They can be divided into two groups.

Group One: Personal

This group is made up of you and things related directly to you—your ideas, beliefs, passions, possessions, hobbies, knowledge, and happiness, etc. This group also includes your spouse or partner, family members, and close friends and neighbors.

Group Two: Professional

The second group consists of things related to your sources of income (your salary or your business interests or other investments) and the people you associate with on a professional basis—co-workers, customers, teammates, associates, and fellow group members.

This process can help you no matter where you are in life. If you are retired, this book may help you find ways to leverage your savings or pension. If you are unemployed, there are ideas here that can be helpful as you begin looking for a way to find employment, create delta, and enjoy a comfortable income. You might also find ideas that help you improve a damaged relationship.

As you create a list of things you value, consider including items from both your personal and professional groups. To create your list, finish the following statement several times: "My life would be much less meaningful without _____." Start by putting yourself at the top of the list.

Things I Value

    1. Myself: _____

    2. _____

    3. _____

    4. _____

    5. _____

    6. _____

7. _____

8. _____

With your two lists complete, you are ready to move to the next steps.

Four Simple Steps

You can follow these steps on your own or with a group. Focus on one value at a time (your focus value) and measure how it impacts one item on your Things I Value list. In the beginning, center your attention on one value for a week and see the delta created on that one item.

Here are the four steps:

1. Choose a focus value from your My Priority Values list.

2. Choose an item from your Things I Value list on which you can apply the focus value.

3. Do one or more of the following ideas to keep you centered on your objective.

    a. Find a picture of something that makes you think of your chosen value and post it in a prominent place—think bathroom mirror, office computer, cell phone wallpaper, car dashboard, etc. You may also elect to add a photo of the chosen item from your Things I Value list.

  b. Find a quote in this book or online that highlights your chosen value. Print your quote and put it where you can read it and reflect upon it multiple times each day. You may also choose a poem or a scripture verse to highlight your chosen value.

  c. Spend a few minutes each day reading or listening to books, podcasts, articles, etc., that are focused on your chosen value.

  d. Seek opportunities during the week to discuss your chosen value with family, friends, and associates.

4. Write down one activity that you will do to create delta for your chosen item from your Things I Value list to emphasize or highlight the chosen value from your My Priority Values list.

> "My intention being to acquire the habitude of all these [13] virtues, I judg'd it would be well not to distract my attention by attempting the whole at once, but to fix it on one of them at a time; and, when I should be master of that, then to proceed to another, and so on, till I should have gone thro' the thirteen; and, as the previous acquisition of some might facilitate the acquisition of certain others, I arrang'd them with that view...."
>
> – Benjamin Franklin, *Benjamin Franklin's Autobiography*

For example, you may choose to make a difference in your small business by emphasizing the value of cheerfulness by 1) sharing a cheerfulness quote each morning in your employee meeting, and/

or by 2) giving a welcoming smile to every customer that walks into your store during an entire week.

The steps above will help make your chosen value a part of your everyday mindset and actions. These words from Nikaya resonate with me. He taught, "Whatever a monk keeps pursuing with his thinking and pondering, that becomes the inclination of his awareness."[5]

Please take time to make a self-assessment of the results of your efforts or report your results to a friend. Was delta created? In what way was delta created for the thing or person(s) you value?

From week to week or month to month, you can choose to focus on one Priority Value and how it changes the things you value. With discipline, this process will, over time, create significant delta for you personally and professionally.

---

5 "Dvedhavitakka Sutta: Two Sorts of Thinking," Majjhima Nikāya 19, trans. Thanissaro Bhikkhu, Access to Insight, https://www.accesstoinsight.org/tipitaka/mn/mn.019.than.html.

Your Values Matter—The "V Effect"

Your values matter in your profession. Your values matter in your life. Your values, strong or weak, influence everything that gives your life meaning, and that influence has a ripple effect seemingly without end. I call that ripple effect the Value Effect or the V Effect, for short. I mentioned it earlier in my conversation with Rick. Let me give you another simple example.

This account is about someone I'll refer to as Jim. Honesty is one of Jim's Priority Values, and since Jim is an honest employee, perhaps his boss recognizes and appreciates his honesty and rewards him financially for it. Through a pay raise or a promotion, Jim financially adds value to himself. That value—honesty—also adds value to something else Jim values, namely his job. Customers return to the company Jim works for because the word is out: Jim is an honest person to work with. Thus, Jim's employer is happier and reaps the benefit of financial delta for her company. It's the ripple effect of positive values—the V Effect. And we should not leave out the V Effect of Jim's honesty outside of work, among his family and friends.

This V Effect can cut both ways. When Julie and I lived in Texas, we had a discussion with a psychologist whose job was to counsel and help people, beginning with a conversation about their moral values. He believed that behavior should match values. He taught us that trouble came when people acted inconsistently with their values.

How does that work? If one of my values is fidelity, but I have an affair, problems arise. If one of my values is patience, but I frequently lose my temper at home and at work, problems arise. If one of my values is love, but I do not accept it or give it, problems arise. The pattern is obvious, and the negative results can be far reaching.

So, what do you do to create a positive V Effect? You elevate your values. You magnify them. You talk about them. You live up to them. And if you see an area where you can improve, you add to or work on the value that is lacking. Then you'll see the V Effect begin to manifest itself in a variety of ways. Your life improves, as do the lives of those around you.

It sounds simple, but it can be harder than it appears. Being willing to take a serious self-inventory, asking yourself how you can change and improve, can be uncomfortable. You can overcome the discomfort and start the process of creating delta in your life in both quantitative and qualitative ways, as you continue to experiment with the proven recommendations.

It will take time and consistent effort. When you decide what you are willing to sacrifice today to get what you want tomorrow, not just for yourself but for those around you, you will improve. When you decide the effort of magnifying or adding to your Priority Values is worth it, you will grow and feel more confident. And never forget: Your Values Matter!

Two Paths

Now that you have completed your lists, calculated your Value Point Average, and are familiar with the V Effect, the following stories, thoughts, and ideas will help increase your VPA and add value by creating delta for the people and things that bring joy and meaning to your life.

I am happy to share my current list of Priority Values. I do this to further motivate myself and empower you to create your own Priority Values list. My list is for my benefit and it is fluid. Please create your own list based on your needs at this time. We may have common elements on our lists but if we don't, that is okay. The remaining chapters of this book highlight my Priority Values as a template for you. They are:

1. Optimism
2. Kindness

3. Gratitude

4. Service

5. Integrity

6. Communication

7. Humility

8. Initiative

If some of these values appear on your My Priority Values list, I hope the chapter on that value will help generate ideas as you increase your value grade and increase your overall VPA. Most of the stories that follow involve adults, and a few are about children, often my own. I invite you to apply the *principle* of the story to yourself or your organization regardless of your age or the age of the story's main character.

The eight values listed above all have personal significance to me. They represent where I am at today. My Priority Values may change tomorrow. That is a normal growth pattern. I should also mention that you don't need to have eight Priority Values. Any number is fine. You decide what fits your situation.

In the future, I plan to spend time writing about and focusing on other values including civility, trust, forgiveness, liberty, abundance, wisdom, preparation, and more. But for our purposes here, I'll focus on the eight Priority Values I've outlined above.

I hope you will take the time to decide what your Priority Values are today and then use The Values Delta Report Cards to motivate yourself in the coming weeks, months, and years. Use this book as a resource each time you need to renew your commitment to the importance of your values and the delta they can create in all areas of your life.

There are two paths to choose from now to help you benefit from the remaining chapters:

Path 1: Continue reading *The Values Delta* chapters (1–8) in order.

OR

Path 2: Review the list of the remaining *The Values Delta* chapters and choose chapters that seem most relevant for you and read them first. Then, read the remaining chapters in the order of your interest level. Each chapter is independent of the others and stands alone. Because of this format, you can also read chapters one by one, focusing on a particular value each week.

Each chapter follows a similar pattern, beginning with stories that illustrate the importance of the highlighted value. Then comes an invitation to grade yourself according to how you feel you are incorporating that value in your life. Also, there are a few practical ideas of how you might choose to be a delta maker as it relates to the value being discussed. Finally, there is a list of related values that you may want to include now, on your list of Priority Values, or down the road.

Thank you for joining me in this quest. Let's move on to Part Two and the eight remaining chapters.

PART TWO

1. The Value of Optimism: Nobody Wears Shoes

I fell in love with woodworking when I was a teenager. My favorite class in high school was wood shop. Forty years later, I still treasure the small dresser I made in that class.

Woodworking brought me so much satisfaction during my teen years that I built a large bookcase and secured it to my bedroom wall above the headboard of my bed. In the center of the bookcase was an 18 by 24 inch space where I hung a framed poem that became the focal point of my bedroom.

If I could remember who introduced these words to me, I would thank him or her because they have had a powerful impact on my life. Author and teacher Christian D. Larson penned "Promise Yourself" over 100 years ago, in 1912.[6]

---

6   Christian D. Larson, *Your Forces and How to Use Them* (Eastford: Martino Fine Books, 2012).

Promise Yourself

- To be so strong that nothing can disturb your peace of mind.

- To talk health, happiness and prosperity to every person you meet.

- To make all your friends feel that there is something special in them.

- To look at the sunny side of everything and make your optimism come true.

- To think only of the best, to work only for the best, and to expect only the best.

- To be just as enthusiastic about the success of others as you are about your own.

- To forget the mistakes of the past and press on to the greater achievements of the future.

- To wear a cheerful countenance at all times and give every living creature you meet a smile.

- To give so much time to the improvement of yourself that you have no time to criticize others.

- To be too large for worry, too noble for anger, too strong for fear, and too happy to permit the presence of trouble.

I have repeated these lines to myself over and over. Although I love each line for different reasons, one line has always stood out above the others: "To look at the sunny side of everything and make your optimism come true."

The words lift me and give me hope. Optimism seems to be in short supply these days. If I could give a gift to the world, I think I would give the gift of optimism.

News headlines make it clear we are suffering from a gross lack of optimism. The question remains: Can an extra dose of optimism change me? Will it create delta personally and professionally for me if I include it on my list of Priority Values?

The Story of Two Travelers

A traveler walking along a dusty road saw a monk tending a small crop near the road. The monk, seeing the traveler, called out, "Good day!" to him, and the traveler nodded in return. The traveler took a few more steps toward the monk and said, "Excuse me, may I ask you a question?"

"Certainly," replied the monk.

The traveler stated that he had been walking from his village in the mountains to the valley and asked the monk. "Can you tell me what it is like in the next village down in the valley?"

> "Optimism is a happiness magnet. If you stay positive, good things and good people will be drawn to you."
> – Mary Lou Retton, Olympic gymnast, Mary Lou Retton's *Gateways to Happiness*

"First," replied the monk, "tell me of your experience in your village in the mountains."

"It was dreadful," the traveler said. "I'm glad to be away from there. The people were mean, and I was never accepted no matter how hard I tried to make friends. The villagers kept to themselves and did not like strangers or newcomers. Will it be the same in the village in the valley?"

"I am sorry to tell you," said the monk, "but I think your experience will be much the same there."

Disappointed, the traveler despondently walked on.

A few hours later another traveler journeyed down the same road and approached the monk.

"I'm on my way to the village in the valley," said the new traveler. "Can you tell me what it is like?"

"Certainly," said the monk. "But first, can you tell me where you have come from?"

"I have walked from the village in the mountains," he answered.

"And how was that village?" the monk asked.

"Wonderful!" the second traveler said. "I would have stayed, but I was already committed to travelling on. I felt as though I was a member of the village family. The elders were my mentors, the young people trusted me, and we laughed and joked together. I am sad to be gone from there. The village in the mountains will always hold special memories for me. But what of the village in the valley?"

"I think you will find it much the same," said the monk. "I wish you well."

"Thank you," the traveler replied as he smiled and journeyed on.

Which traveler are you? If you are the first traveler, there is still hope. With little effort being made to be more optimistic, a big difference will be evident.

When Optimism Meets Odor

My friend Allen Kreutzkamp helped me choose to live the value of optimism more fully.

I first met Allen early in my real estate investing career. He had recently earned his real estate license, was dating a wonderful woman, and it appeared that a wedding announcement was imminent.

He called me one day and said, "Devin, I've found the woman of my dreams. We're planning to be married soon, and I want to take my new bride on a magical honeymoon. But I have a small problem. I'm out of cash right at the moment. I need $5,000. I have a house under contract to purchase, and I wonder if you would like to take it off my hands. For $5,000 you can take over my contract."

I trusted Allen. He always found good investments, so I agreed to tour the house.

I took one look at the yard and the exterior of the house, and my heart sank. It was all a mess. I wanted to help Allen, but I almost drove away before even looking inside. When I entered, it smelled like urine. The kitchen ceiling was falling in, and garbage was strewn all over. I couldn't wait to leave! I wanted to rush home, take a hot shower, and call Allen to say the deal was off.

But I stayed. I picked a spot in the house where the ceiling looked solid, stood there, and waited for Allen. I wondered, "What could Allen be thinking in showing me this house? It's a scary place! Why would I want to buy this house?"

> "One of the things I learned the hard way was that it doesn't pay to get discouraged. Keeping busy and making optimism a way of life can restore your faith in yourself."
> – Lucille Ball, *The Times Book of Quotations*, p. 520

When Allen arrived, we walked through the house—very carefully.

He shared his ideas of what could be done with the house. The bad smell could be removed, and the size and location were ideal. The zoning would allow the house to become a duplex; one family on the main floor, and one in the basement.

Slowly, I caught Allen's vision. I saw beyond the smell. I saw beyond the garbage. I realized the deteriorating roof could be fixed; I saw potential. Allen's sense of optimism was contagious.

That lesson stayed with me. In real estate, there are things some people cannot see past: ugly carpet, an overgrown lawn, a broken window, even though these things are fixable. Cosmetic problems can be resolved fairly quickly with some sweat and a few dollars. With a little time to clean up the yard and install new carpet and windows, you can change a wreck to a home. Because of Allen's optimism, I *now* choose to see beyond the problems. I choose to see the solutions. I choose to see the opportunities. I'm striving to be optimistic in all aspects of my life.

The good news—actually, the great news—was that the house came with an adjacent lot. Though it was full of junk, underneath it all was more potential. The lot was big enough that a new home could be built on it. That was all I needed to hear. I was sold!

Allen had the house under contract for $75,000. I gave him $5,000, assumed his position, and closed on the house and the lot. As part of the deal, we had an agreement with the owner that we wouldn't close until everything on the lot next door was removed and all the debris in the house was cleared out. The owner held up his part of the agreement, and the property was transformed.

Soon after closing, we started on the interior of the house, cleaning, painting, fixing, and installing new carpet. With new siding, new roof supports and shingles, we invested a large sum of money on top of the purchase price. We then sold the house, made a nice profit, and we still owned the empty lot. Allen's optimistic vision and knowledge helped me overcome my fears and created delta for my real estate company in an easily quantifiable way. But the experience was more impactful in a qualitative way—my vision had been changed for the better.

The Twelve Spies

Unfortunately, pessimism has a long life and never seems to die.

Let's take a look back.

Thousands of years ago, in preparation for entering the Promised Land, the Lord commanded Moses to send 12 spies to search the land. Moses followed the command and sent one leader from each of the 12 tribes of Israel. Moses was specific as to their duty:

> Get you up this way southward and go up into the mountain: and see the land, what it is; and the people that dwelleth therein, whether they be strong or weak, few or many; and what the land is that they dwell in, whether they be good or bad; and what cities they be that they dwell in, whether in tents, or in strong holds; and what the land is, whether it be fat or lean, whether there be wood therein, or not. And be ye of good courage and bring of the fruit of the land.[7]

The spies spent 40 days in the land and reported back to Moses and all of Israel that the land was indeed a land of "milk and honey"[8] but warned that the people who dwelled in the land were strong. In fact, they were giants!

---

7   "Numbers 13:17–20," King James Bible (KJV) online, https://www.kingjamesbibleonline.org/ Numbers-13-17/.

8   "Numbers 13:27," KJV, https://www.kingjamesbibleonline.org/Numbers-13-27/.

"And the cities are walled, and very great."[9] When it was suggested that they possess the land, ten of the spies said: "We be not able to go up against the people; for they are stronger than we."[10] The giants that possessed the land would view them as little more than grasshoppers.[11]

Two of the spies, Joshua and Caleb, wanted to return to the Promised Land. They spoke to the children of Israel, saying, "The land, which we passed through to search it, is an exceeding good land. If the Lord delight in us, then he will bring us into this land, and give it us; a land which floweth with milk and honey."[12] Upon hearing this speech, the people insisted that Joshua and Caleb be stoned.[13] As a punishment for their attitude, the children of Israel wandered in the wilderness for 40 years as the Lord promised that "surely they shall not see the land which I sware unto their fathers, neither shall any of them that provoked me see it."[14]

The voice of optimism was silenced. Fear won. Is a similar battle warring in your life or in your company today?

Shoes

A shoe manufacturer sent two salesmen to explore the African continent and report back regarding the potential for the shoe industry there.

---

9   "Numbers 13:28," KJV, https://www.kingjamesbibleonline.org/Numbers-13-28/.

10   "Numbers 13:31," KJV, https://www.kingjamesbibleonline.org/Numbers-13-31/.

11   "Numbers 13:33," KJV, https://www.kingjamesbibleonline.org/Numbers-13-33/.

12   "Numbers 14:8," KJV, https://www.kingjamesbibleonline.org/Numbers-14-8/.

13   "Numbers 14:10," KJV, https://www.kingjamesbibleonline.org/Numbers-14-10/.

14   "Numbers 14:23, KJV, https://www.kingjamesbibleonline.org/Numbers-14-23/.

Upon their return, the first salesman reported to the shoe manufacturer. "We shouldn't waste our time," the salesman said. "There is no potential for us in Africa. Nobody there wears shoes!"

The second salesman reported: "We need to expand there, the sooner the better! There is massive potential in Africa. Nobody there wears shoes!"[15]

"Nobody there wears shoes." One situation viewed two different ways. One salesman chose to see problems and disadvantages. The other chose to see opportunities and future benefits.

Which salesman do you identify with? What is your outlook on life? Positive or negative? Do you recognize how your outlook invites or eliminates opportunity?

The Attraction of Optimism

Meg Whitman was a division general manager at the toy company Hasbro. She considered her job to be exciting. Her sons participated in the toy testing program and she was earning serious parenting bonus points. They played with new Nerf guns and Star Wars gear before their friends could buy them.[16]

Still, she was on the lookout for new opportunities, and her executive recruiter recommended she meet with the founders of eBay. Although she was skeptical of the tiny company with an odd webpage, she was instantly attracted to the optimism of the company.

The founder of eBay attributed the company's success to "the idea that most people are basically good and that users could be trusted to do the right thing most of the time."[17] Whitman loved this concept.

---

15 Fick, *Entrepreneurship in Africa: A Study of Success* (Santa Barbara: Praeger, 2002), 56.

16 Meg Whitman, *The Power of Many: Values for Success in Business and in Life* (New York: Currency, 2010), 14.

17 Ibid, 18.

She recognized that many companies take a pessimistic view on the future, so this focus on optimism was a refreshing—and needed— shift in values:

> I know there are those who think trust or values were just happy sidecars to a clever and effective business model at a unique time and place. And I can assure you that there are those in boardrooms and on Wall Street who simply reject the idea that people are basically good. They see the business world as a zero-sum game where for one person to win, another must lose. They believe that customer service is important but that it has nothing to do with respect or a belief in the goodness of people....[18]

The amazing success of eBay is one example of how a good idea energized with optimism can "change the world." Values matter, and optimism may be the key value to help you improve your life in material ways.

"No one wants to follow a pessimist."
– Bob Iger, Chairman of Disney, *The Ride of a Lifetime*

The Drought

One story I've heard involves a small community of farmers who were in a quandary because they faced a drought that seemed to con- tinue for an eternity. Rain was important to keep their crops healthy and sustain the townspeople's way of life. As the problem became more acute, a local pastor called a prayer meeting to ask for rain.

---

18 Whitman, *The Power of Many,* 27–28.

As the pastor walked to the front of the church to begin the meeting, he noticed his parishioners were chatting across the aisles and socializing with friends. When he reached the front, his thoughts were on quieting the attendees and starting the meeting.

His eyes scanned the crowd as he asked for quiet. He noticed an 11-year-old girl sitting quietly in the front row, her face beaming with excitement. Next to her, poised and ready for use, was a bright red umbrella. The little girl's innocence made the pastor smile as he realized how much faith she possessed. No one else in the congregation had brought an umbrella.

All came to pray for rain, but the little girl had come expecting God to deliver rain.

Business Is Great!

I enjoy the story about a landscape gardener who ran his family's business, which had been operational for multiple generations. Customers liked coming to the nursery because the staff was happy.

Many people assumed the happiness of the workers came from the success of the business, but this was not the case. This nursery had experienced tough times along with the good like most businesses. Regardless of some bumps in the road, the owner always wore a big lapel badge that reported: "Business Is Great!" No matter what happened, the owner proudly wore the badge.

Many who saw the badge for the first time asked, "What's so great about business?" Others commented that their own businesses were struggling or that they were personally miserable or stressed.

In response to this negativity, the owner shared the positive aspects of business: meeting and talking to different people every day, taking on and solving new challenges, working somewhere that was healthy and relaxed, finishing hard jobs, or even learning something new.

His list of advantages went on and on. No matter how miserable someone may have felt before the conversation started, they would usually end up feeling happier after just a couple of minutes listening to the infectious enthusiasm and positivity of the owner."

It is impossible to quantify or measure the impact of an optimistic attitude like the one this business owner displayed but consider how the V Effect might have been evident as customers left this business, then interacted with others. Since optimism is infectious, let's spread it far and wide.

I Don't Have to Be Like Mike

A word of caution. Often, we lean toward pessimistic thoughts as we compare ourselves to others. We begin to feel we don't measure up. How would you feel if you compared yourself to the greatest basketball player of all time?

During the 1984 Olympic trials, I competed against Michael Jordan.[19] I was amazed by his quickness and skill set. I relished the opportunity to compare myself against the best.

One afternoon after a workout, I rode in the elevator with Michael. I'm 6'7" tall, and he's 6'6" tall. Individually, we stand out. Together, we really stood out. The elevator dinged, the doors opened, and an elderly lady joined us. She looked up and up at us and asked with a smile, "And who are you two boys?"

"I am Devin Durrant," I answered with a smile. I continued in a self-deprecating style and said, "I am a nobody. But this is the great Michael Jordan." He was great even at that point in his life.

The three of us had a little conversation as the elevator clicked through the floors. I've thought about that conversation many times

---

19 Curry Kirkpatrick, "It Was Trial By Fire," *Sports Illustrated* Vault, April 30, 1984, https://vault. si.com/vault/1984/04/30/it-was-trial-by-fire.

since. The woman's question was so simple, so sincere: "Who are you?"

I know exactly who I am, and I'm happy with who I am. Would I want to be Michael Jordan? I admit, I covet his skills, his quick hands, his athleticism, his mindset, and his multifaceted abilities, but I am happy being me. I don't want to be like Mike, as a popular marketing campaign suggested years ago.[20]

Comparing myself to others like Michael Jordan can be as corrosive to my soul as acid is to everything it touches. There may be a time and a place for comparison. I saw this when I was an athlete, and I see it now as a businessperson. Look around and see who you are competing with on your team, in your league, or in your market since it can cause you to try harder and be better. But never let competition become a vice—never let it lead you to a place of pessimism. With clear Priority Values, you can look at the people around you and feel optimistic and content knowing you are enough.

The Greatest of All

I wouldn't feel comfortable leaving this discussion of optimism without highlighting He who best demonstrated optimism always, even in the face of adversity. During the last week of Jesus Christ's life, he was betrayed by a close associate (Judas), denied by a dear friend (Peter), and rejected and mocked by many. You may have had a period of time or experience that reminded you of the adversity Jesus faced. This is what He said during his troubling times: "In the world ye shall have tribulation: but be of good cheer; I have overcome the world."[21] As a result of Christ's atoning sacrifice, the

---

20 Darren Rovell, "Famed 'Be Like Mike' Gatorade ad Debuted 25 years ago," ESPN, August 8, 2016, https://www.espn.com/nba/story/_/id/17246999/michael-jordan-famous-mike-gatorade-commercial-debuted-25-years-ago-monday.

21 "John 16:33," KJV, https://www.kingjamesbibleonline.org/John-Chapter-16/#33.

doors to exaltation are open to all of us. There is no greater reason for optimism and "good cheer" than that.

Optimism Grade

How are you doing today with the value of optimism? What grade do you give yourself? Here are a few ideas that might help you make delta with your optimism.

Optimism Tools

Take a step up on the Optimism Scale. For example, if someone says to you, "The sky is beautiful," what is your first thought?

The optimistic person says, "I wholeheartedly agree with you, and the green mountains are such a nice complement to the blue sky."

The pessimistic person responds by saying something like, "It might be beautiful now, but I bet it is going to rain later today. I hate it when it rains."

Let's try another one. If someone says to you, "Ryan is a kind and thoughtful person," what is your first thought?

The optimist says, "Another thing I appreciate about Ryan is his judgment. He always seems to make good decisions."

The pessimist responds with words similar to these, "He is not very kind to me. And on top of that, he acts like a know-it-all. I'd call him 'Mr. Arrogant.'"

And last if someone says to you, "Thank you for helping with the project. Your contribution was critical to our success!" What is your first thought?

The optimistic person says, "You are very welcome. I really appreciate the confidence I felt from you and the independence you gave me as I worked."

The pessimistic person responds with words similar to these, "Well, I am not sure I really did anything to help. As a matter of fact, I wish I weren't so lazy when it comes to team projects."

Are you hearing your voice in any of these examples?

Think about the people in your life: family members, friends, work associates, neighbors. If you were to label each of them as either an optimist or a pessimist, who would fit in which camp? Who do you prefer to spend time with? My guess is that you spend as much time as possible with the positive group, and as little time as possible with those who live life in the negative zone. If someone were to put you in an optimist or pessimist camp, which one would it be?

Let's pause for a quick self-assessment. Write an "X" on the scale below at the point you think represents your outlook on life today.

The Optimism Scale

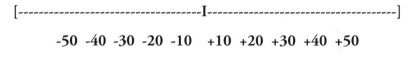

-50 -40 -30 -20 -10   +10 +20 +30 +40 +50

Pessimist - Negativity   Optimist - Positivity

I showed the Optimism Scale to my daughter Deanna and to my wife Julie. Deanna placed herself at +10 and Julie placed herself at +20. I asked them about an interaction they thought they could have handled better. If they scored further to the right on The Optimism Scale, what would have been different?

Deanna answered quite honestly, "I could have been more enthusiastic about helping you with this survey. When you asked if I would help, I only said 'Maybe.'"

Julie said she could have responded more graciously when I offered her a book to read that I had enjoyed. "I told you it was not the type of book I thought I would like."

I appreciate their candor. It's clear we can all find room for improvement on The Optimism Scale.

If the outlook of your life currently leans toward the negative, don't feel guilty. Instead, take action and change.

According to an article in Prevention.com by Jane Meredith Adams, pessimism is an emotional defense mechanism. "If you keep your expectations low enough, you won't be crushed when things don't work out."[22]

Adams continues, "But new research has revealed that [a pessimistic] tendency...doesn't merely ruin a good time and prevent you from making friends. It seems that it's a bad strategy by about every measure. Optimists, it turns out, do better in most avenues of life, whether it's work, school, sports, or relationships. They get depressed less often than pessimists do, make more money, and have happier marriages."[23]

A better life, more money, happier relationships? Clearly optimism can create delta in most everything you value. How can you generate more optimism? How can you increase your score on The Optimism Scale? You have the answer to that question within yourself. Are you ready to make it happen? It may take some time and practice, but the effort will be worth it. The delta created by being more positive is proven to be life changing.

---

22 Jane Meredith Adams, "6 Easy Ways to Be a Whole Lot More Optimistic about Everything," Prevention, December 7, 2017, https://www.prevention.com/life/g20474730/the-pessi-mists-guide-to-being-optimistic/.

23 Ibid.

Take another look at your place on The Optimism Scale. If you are not satisfied with where you are, if you would like to move to the right, use the ideas in this chapter, draft a plan and commit to being more optimistic. You can do it. Delta is added as you move farther to the right.

Is optimism a value you want to focus on? If not, you might consider some close cousins from our Values List in Appendix 1:

- Accuracy
- Achievement
- Cheerfulness
- Confidence
- Eagerness
- Enthusiasm
- Innovation
- Maturity
- Pleasantness
- Vision

2. The Value of Kindness: I Like Your Hat

I read the following account on BleacherReport.com.[24] It was shared by Coach Paul "Bear" Bryant at a Touchdown Club meeting. This story left an indelible impression on me. Coach Bryant started his story this way:

> I had just been named the new head coach at Alabama and was off in my old car down in South Alabama recruiting a prospect who was supposed to have been a pretty good player, and I was having trouble finding the place.
>
> Getting hungry, I spied an old cinder block building with a small sign out front that simply said 'Restaurant.' I pull up, go in, and every head in the place turns to stare at me. Seems I'm the only

---

24 Larry Burton, "It Don't Cost Nothin' to Be Nice," Bleacher Report, September 26, 2008, https://bleacherreport.com/articles/61880-it-dont-cost-nothin-to-be-nice.

white fella in the place. But the food smelled good, so I skip a table and go up to a cement bar and sit.

A big ole man in a tee shirt and cap comes over and says, 'What do you need?' I told him I needed lunch and what did they have today? He says, 'You probably won't like it here, today we're having chitlins, collard greens, and black-eyed peas with cornbread. I'll bet you don't even know what chitlins are, do you?'

I looked him square in the eye and said, 'I'm from Arkansas, I've probably eaten a mile of them. Sounds like I'm in the right place.'

As the lunch was ending, the restaurant owner asked Coach Bryant what brought him to the area. He explained that he was the new coach at the University of Alabama and he was in the area to visit a prized recruit and his coach.

Coach Bryant then leaves a nice tip and is about to leave when the owner asks him for a photograph he could hang up to show he had been there.

Coach Bryant explained to him that he didn't have any photos yet, but he wrote the owner's name and address on a napkin and told him he would send him one later. Later than afternoon, Coach Bryant met the recruit he was hoping to see, but he was not impressed.

He continued his story.

I had wasted a day, or so I thought. When I got back to Tuscaloosa late that night, I took that napkin from my shirt pocket and put it under my keys so I wouldn't forget it. Back then I was excited that anybody would want a picture of me.

The next day we found a picture and I wrote on it, 'Thanks for the best lunch I've ever had.'

Several years passed and Coach Bryant again found himself in that area to scout a highly regarded offensive lineman.

Y'all remember, (and I forget the name, but it's not important to the story), well anyway, he's got two friends going to Auburn and he tells me he's got his heart set on Auburn too, so I leave empty-handed and go on to see some others while I'm down there.

Two days later, I'm in my office in Tuscaloosa and the phone rings, and it's this kid who just turned me down, and he says, 'Coach, do you still want me at Alabama?' And I said, 'Yes, I sure do.' And he says okay, he'll come. And I say, 'Well son, what changed your mind?'

And he said, 'When my grandpa found out that I had a chance to play for you and said no, he pitched a fit and told me I wasn't going nowhere but Alabama and wasn't playing for nobody but you. He thinks a lot of you and has ever since y'all met.'

> "Let no one ever come to you without leaving better and happier. Be the living expression of God's kindness—kindness in your face, kindness in your eyes, kindness in your smile, kindness in your warm greeting."
> – Mother Teresa, in Susan Conroy, *Mother Teresa's Lessons of Love and Secrets of Sanctity*

Well, I didn't know his granddad from Adam's housecat, so I asked him who his granddaddy was, and he said, 'You probably don't remember him, but you ate in his restaurant your first year at Alabama and you sent him a picture that he's had hung in that place ever since. That picture's his pride and joy, and he still tells everybody about the day that Bear Bryant came in and had chitlins with him.'

'My grandpa said that when you left there, he never expected you to remember him or to send him that picture, but you kept your word to him, and to Grandpa that's everything. He said you could teach me more than football and I had to play for a man like you, so I guess I'm going to.'

Coach Bryant could hardly believe what he was hearing from this prized recruit. He finished the story this way:

I learned that the lessons my mama taught me were always right. It don't cost nuthin' to be nice. It don't cost nuthin' to do the right thing most of the time, and it costs a lot to lose your good name by breaking your word to someone.

When I went back to sign that boy, I looked up his Grandpa, and he's still running that place, but it looks a lot better now; and he didn't have chitlins that day, but he had some ribs that would make Dreamland proud, and I made sure I posed for a lot of pictures; and don't think I didn't leave some new ones for him, too, along with a signed football.

I made it clear to all my assistants to keep this story and these lessons in mind when they're out on the road. If you remember anything else from me, remember this. It really doesn't cost anything to be nice, and the rewards can be unimaginable.

Thank you, Coach Bryant, for sharing this memorable and meaningful experience from your life!

Generally, kindness doesn't add value quantitatively, but it certainly adds qualitative value. Here are some questions to ponder. How can kindness create delta for me in my profession? In my home? How might the V Effect of kindness play out in my world?

To start your journey exploring the value of kindness, think about yesterday. Specifically, think back to your interactions with others.

Did you work on a new project with a coworker? Did you talk with a parent on the phone? Did you answer a client's question? Did you help a child with homework?

How would you rate each interaction? Is there something you could have done differently to feel happier with each interaction?

Choose Kindness

In R. J. Palacio's fictional book, *Wonder*, Palacio introduces readers to her main character, August, or Auggie for short. Auggie was born with a facial deformation so extreme that his doctor fainted onto the floor when Auggie was born. "I won't describe what I look like," Auggie explains in the book. "Whatever you're thinking, it's probably worse."[25]

Auggie, who has always been homeschooled by his mother, bravely decides to go to school. Kindness is a theme Auggie reverts back to again and again during his school year. In fact, when he goes to English class, Auggie reads a simple rule on the board:

When given the choice between being right or being kind, choose to be kind.

After a bumpy but good year, Auggie joins the rest of his class at a graduation ceremony. The principal, Mr. Tushman, gives one last speech where the theme of kindness again is reiterated.

Mr. Tushman tells the audience:

"It's not enough to be kind. One should be kinder than needed. Why I love that…concept, is that it reminds me that we carry with us, as human beings, not just the capacity to be kind, but the very choice of kindness."

---

25   R. J. Palacio, Wonder (New York: Alfred A. Knopf, 2012).

Kinder than needed. A beautiful mantra to live by and one to think about when you begin a new project with a coworker or talk with a parent on the phone or answer a client's question or help a child with homework. By adding a kindness delta to these situations, the light in each interaction increases—most people will notice that you are striving to be a little kinder than needed. Imagine the extent of the kindness V Effect.

> "If I can stop one heart from breaking,
> I shall not live in vain:
>
> If I can ease one life the aching,
> Or cool one pain,
> Or help one fainting robin
> Unto his nest again,
> I shall not live in vain."
>
> – Emily Dickinson, *Hope is the Thing With Feathers*

Clive Winn(er)

I met Clive Winn when I worked at WordPerfect Corporation. Clive added value at work through his smile and congenial personality. He always had something upbeat to say. He was consistently joyful and warm to everyone inside and outside the company. He understood the values delta better than anyone I knew during that time. If WordPerfect Corporation had asked for a vote, Clive would have been voted the Most Loved Employee because he made work a more enjoyable experience with his cheerful nature and unwavering kindness. I believe that one's work environment impacts one's productivity. I saw evidence of that as I watched Clive interact with others. Everyone under Clive's leadership influence seemed to feel an extra measure of loyalty and wanted to give a bit more to their jobs than was required.

Does Clive's example of leadership remind you of anyone? Who came to mind as you read the story of Clive Winn(er) and his kindness? Is there someone like Clive at your company? Is it you? What's stopping you from being that person?

The Power to Change the World

My family decided to move from Louisville, Kentucky, to Provo, Utah, when I was a teenager. I had no trouble transitioning into my new high school, Provo High, but my sister, Kathryn, struggled to adjust. She felt lonely, without friends, and lost in a sea of faces. She went home to eat lunch so she didn't have to sit alone in the cafeteria. One day a classmate invited Kathryn to eat lunch with her and introduced Kathryn to her friends. My sister adjusted more easily with the support of those new friends.

> "Kindness is a language which the deaf can hear and the blind can see."
>
> – Christian Nestell Bovee, *Thoughts, Feelings, and Fancies*

Perhaps you think the little things you do will not have big consequences, but the V Effect and a little effort goes a long way. A simple invitation to eat lunch changed Kathryn's life. She went from feeling alone to belonging to a group of supportive friends. Kathryn went on to do similar acts of kindness for others who were in her former shoes.

The story doesn't stop there. A similar act of kindness a generation later became a source of strength for my oldest daughter, Emily, who also had to switch to a new high school mid-stream. She did so just before her senior year. She understood well her aunt's experience.

Emily was a graduation speaker at Provo High School in 2002. She shared her Aunt Kathryn's story and related it to her own life:

> I spent a good part of the first couple of weeks in our new house depressed and lonely. Then, one day, I met three beautiful girls who lived close to my new residence. They began making daily visits to my house or calling me on the phone and drew me into their circle of friendship. They provided me with the strength I needed to make it to this day: graduation with Provo High School's class of 2002.
>
> You may wonder how these small acts of kindness changed the world. They didn't change your world, you say. Well, they changed my aunt's world, and they most definitely changed my world. One small act completely altered the way we felt about life and the way we felt about the world around us.

For my Emily, new friends came along through simple acts of kindness, and it made all the difference for her. When you resolve to be kinder, your small and simple acts will change the things you value for the better.

Be Kind to the Server

My second-oldest daughter, Laura, showed kindness several years ago when she and eight of her friends went out for breakfast at a local restaurant. After they finished eating, they looked around and realized they were leaving an extra-large and messy collection of plates and glasses and silverware and used napkins for the server to clean up, so they were prompted to leave an extra cash bonus along with a standard tip.

The group talked for a few minutes at the door of the restaurant and when they were about to leave, another server approached them.

Laura worried for a few seconds that perhaps she was in trouble for the mess.

Instead, the server shared that her coworker had been praying all morning to make enough money to pay her rent. Laura and her friends helped answer that prayer. They showed more kindness than was necessary and were blessed to see the V Effect in action. Laura and her friends nearly floated home; they felt wonderful.

Number One Christian

My father shared an experience he had during his military service in the Army as a private first class in Korea. He did not speak Korean and had only lived there a few months. He came to love the people he worked with who only understood limited English. In order to overcome the language barrier, my father had what he called "a middle language."

"This a Number One Jeep," he'd tell his colleague if he had a good Jeep that was running smoothly.

"Ah, Number One!" the colleague would say.

If their Jeep were struggling, the colleague would have a different rank: "Number 10."

"Ah, Number 10," my father would say.

They used their scale to rank everything. Number One was the best.

One night in the mess hall, a Korean man who was working as a waiter came up to my father with a tray of food. Waiters normally only served higher ranks, such as corporals, but the Korean waiter set down the tray of food in front of my father and said, "I serve you. You a Number One Christian."[26]

---

26 George Durrant, Scones for the Heart: 184 Inspiring Morsels of Wit and Wisdom to Warm Your Soul (Springville: Bonneville Books, 2002), 251-253.

Apparently, the Korean waiter had seen my dad giving way to Korean workers on the narrow dirt paths between army buildings. Koreans normally stepped off the paths to let Americans pass, but my father decided to always be the first to get off the path and let the Koreans pass. This tradition, he said, "was only a little thing, but I felt good in doing it."

In a land where Christianity had just been introduced, my father's example of conducting himself with kindness made an impression on the Korean workers and a deeper one on my dad. After his experience with the Korean waiter, my father reflected, "I will always hear those words. It was the greatest compliment that has ever been paid to me. 'I serve you. You a Number One Christian.' Oh, how I'd like to be that. I think that became one of my goals, just to see if I could become a Number One Christian."

My father is now 90 years old. I have been a first-hand witness to most of his life and I can say with certainty that he has truly been a Number One Christian. Many people have shared stories with me of my father's kindness to them and the difference it made in their lives. He was particularly keen at remembering names—a small and simple gesture—when most would have long forgotten.

"I Like Your Hat"

Macey, a six-year old girl, shared joy on a hot afternoon at a theme park in Virginia. Macey's older sister was brave and daring and was off to ride a roller coaster. Macey stayed behind on a small bench with her mom.

As they waited, an older woman joined them on the bench. The older woman was wearing a floppy hat and mismatched clothes. The mother noticed Macey staring at the woman and worried about what her daughter might say.

Macey struck up a conversation. Leaning across her mom, she looked at the woman and said, "I like your hat!"

Four small kind words that spread joy across the woman's face.

As you resolve to be kinder in your life, you will impact others with your thoughtful words and selfless deeds. The joy shared through kindness will come back to you in multiples.

Kindness Grade

How do you rate yourself today with the value of kindness? What grade do you give yourself? The following kindness tools are designed to help you create delta as you lift your level of kindness.

Kindness Tools

Think of your recent interactions with a neighbor, a coworker, a spouse, and a child. How might you have been kinder in each instance? Simple reflection on past actions can shed light on ways to be more kind in the future.

Consider this thought from my wife on kindness. She experienced a time when she saw a good friend, and immediately thought to herself, "Her hair looks terrible today." Realizing what she was doing, she asked herself, "Why am I feeling insecure today?" She remembered she had not washed her own hair in a while, and suddenly her friend's hair didn't look so bad. As a result of that experience, whenever Julie has unkind feelings toward another person, she quickly asks herself why she is feeling insecure. It has helped her become a kinder person.

I am a very competitive person and I find I am least kind when I am competing. Think about and avoid situations that tend to bring out less than the best in you.

My family loves to play board games and card games. I realized a long time ago that I am better off observing their games from a distance. The greater the distance the more kind I am. I'm happy to report I'm making progress in this area.

We all experience times when someone is unkind to us. In those situations, consider setting a goal with your family or coworkers to invent reasons why someone was unkind to them. Over dinner or another set time, have each family member tell about a situation where someone was unkind to them. Ask the next person to complete the sentence, "Oh! It's okay. I think they were unkind because they were _____." If someone cut you off on your way to work, or didn't open a door for you, it could be that they were frustrated for being late to their daughter's piano recital. After three days of this exercise, assess how you feel about others when they are unkind to you. It might help your perspective to change for the better.

When we are kind, life feels more peaceful, joyful, and satisfying. No downside to being kind has been discovered. In our home, we often invited our children to "concentrate on kindness." In summary, choose kindness and be kinder than needed.

Here are a few more values that share common ground with kindness from the Values List in Appendix 1:

- Acceptance
- Affection
- Caring
- Compassion
- Courtesy
- Warmth
- Love
- Meekness

- Respect
- Welcoming

3. The Value of Gratitude: A $10,000 Raise

In 1984, I was invited to travel to New York City to participate in the NBA Draft because it appeared I would be selected early, possibly middle to late first round. I hoped that would indeed be the case.

Name after name was called and I started to feel nervous, and a little worried. I was not alone. My wife sat in the old Salt Palace in Salt Lake City, tears coursing down her face, as teams selected their players and I was passed up again and again. The feelings of rejection I felt in elementary school when I was not chosen for a playground game of basketball were back. I was older. I was taller. I was smarter. But the emotions of rejection were the same.

Before the draft, I heard that Utah, Phoenix, and Cleveland were all interested in me. The Utah Jazz had the 16th pick. Many people predicted the Jazz would select me if I were still available. But the Jazz chose a relatively unknown player from Gonzaga University, John

Stockton. People shouted their disappointment when his name was announced, first with gasps, then outright boos. Critics gradually forgave the Jazz brass for what turned out to be one of the best draft picks they ever made.

The Utah Jazz didn't pick me, nor did the team after that, or the team after that.

There I sat in the Big Apple, on the verge of being selected to play in the NBA, the best basketball league on the planet. My NBA dream was minutes away from coming true. I should have been filled with feelings of gratitude, but I wasn't. The first round of the draft ended, and I felt like a failure.

The anxiety of the moment was crushing. Finally, relief came as I was selected in the second round by the Indiana Pacers. I was the first pick of the second round—the 25th overall pick. I had made it to the NBA!

While I played for the Indiana Pacers, I should have been overwhelmed with feelings of gratitude. This was it! Everything I worked toward for years. But I struggled. My confidence was slipping away.

> "The unthankful heart...discovers no mercies; but let the thankful heart sweep through the day, and as the magnet finds the iron, so it will find, in every hour, some heavenly blessings."
> – Henry Ward Beecher, *Life Thoughts*, 1858

The Indiana Pacers waived me during my second training camp, and part of me was relieved. I never felt I played to my potential with that team.

The Phoenix Suns gave me new life when they claimed me after I cleared waivers. I loved playing for the Suns. I played some of my best basketball with them during training camp and even scored 27 points in one pre-season game. I was feeling confident and successful again, but I was released after just four games of the regular season with the Suns. The first NBA player from behind the Iron Curtain was to take my place. His name was Georgi Glouchkov from Bulgaria.

Those were difficult days. In a matter of months, I went from being adored while playing at Brigham Young University to being forgotten in the NBA. I was young and burdened with disappointment. My days as a professional basketball player seemed to be coming to a close.

A New Beginning

Now, I had only one goal: *provide for my family*. I certainly did not feel grateful during that time of upheaval, change, and transition. Maybe you have had similar feelings at one point in your life. It was clear this was not just a struggle for me. It impacted my wife and daughter, too. If something good was going to come from this, it was up to me to make it happen.

It is easy to feel entitled and to try to avoid responsibility, thinking it's up to someone else, like our parents or government, to look out for us. It is also easy to forget that we often have the ability to fix our own problems. When we experience a tough break, how will we respond? We tend to forget to be grateful for what we have while overemphasizing what we are lacking.

With my NBA experience in the rear view mirror, I looked at options to play in Europe. A good opportunity opened up in Spain when a team manager there noticed an article on me in *Sports Illustrated*. The team manager mentioned to the club's leaders that I spoke Spanish as a result of living in Spain for two years as a missionary. One thing led to another and I ended up playing basketball in Spain for two seasons. Not only had I lived there previously, but Julie had studied there during her college days. We both loved being back in Spain and are very grateful for the friends and memories we made in that beautiful country.

I later played for six weeks in France. After two weeks the coach was fired because we were losing. I was released soon after because we were still losing. Julie smiled, and told me it was time to get a "real job." Actually, it was time to leave basketball behind. After showing signs of having star potential, leading the NCAA in scoring for much of my senior year and being named to All-America lists with players like Michael Jordan, Patrick Ewing, Sam Perkins, and Chris Mullin, my NBA career was over almost as soon as it began, and now I was looking for a job.

I had to rebuild, and it was not easy. It felt nearly impossible at the time for me to embrace a spirit of gratitude. It wasn't one of my values.

Except for the time I had spent as a missionary, my entire identity was related to basketball. And now I needed to move on from basketball.

I thought of the possibility of investing in real estate. In between seasons in Europe, Julie and I lived in my older brother's basement. Perusing his bookshelf one day, I found a book on real estate investment.

Finding that book was serendipitous. After reading *Creating Wealth* by Robert Allen,[27] I was so excited I could not sleep. I had found a new path. I had found a pursuit, a profession I thought I could enjoy.

---

27 Robert G. Allen, *Creating Wealth: Retire in Ten Years Using Allen's Seven Principles of Wealth* (New York: Free Press, 2006).

When I was young, I mowed lawns and cleaned office buildings for a few dollars in pay. The concept of improving a property to increase its value was familiar to me. But now, as an adult, it was on a much bigger scale. The idea that I could buy a house or an apartment building, mow the lawn, trim the bushes, paint the walls, and make a few thousand dollars caught my attention. I wanted to learn more.

I attended real estate seminars. Groups came to town, selling the idea of financial freedom. I loved listening to the success stories of the speakers. One of my favorites was told by Wright Thurston. He discussed how he generated monthly cash flow of $17,000 from apartments he owned in Alaska. Stories like that were enticing. My goal moved from providing for my family to the idea of financial freedom. In 1989, I bought my first investment property. I was on a new path, and I was grateful and excited to pursue a new dream.

It was time to start over—to develop a Devin Durrant away from basketball. I welcomed the challenge and was glad not to be alone. I had a wife at my side who was supportive of my new direction. In basketball, my teammates and I learned more from the games we lost than from the games we won. It was time for a sharp learning curve, and I excitedly accepted this difficult change in our lives.

We All Want More

On the radio many years ago, I heard a discussion of the term "wealth." Listeners that made $30,000 a year were invited to call in.

The hosts asked, "Do you want to make more money?"

The resounding response was "Yes!" They then asked, "How much more would be enough?"

"$10,000," the callers answered. "If I made $40,000 a year, life would be easier. My finances would not be such a struggle."

People who made $40,000 were invited to call in, and the hosts asked if they wanted to make more money and what would be enough? "$50,000," they said. "If I made $50,000 a year, life would be easier. My finances would not be such a struggle."

And on it went. The people who made $50,000 wanted to make $60,000. The people who made $60,000 wanted to make $70,000.

The callers would never be satisfied and would never reach a level where they experienced financial freedom. They would always be a $10,000 raise away from the perfect salary. Their satisfaction was drained from them as they constantly reached for more.

In Spain, I learned a little song entitled "Todos Queremos Más."[28] Translated to English, the title would be "We All Want More." It goes something like this:

We all want more. We all want more.

He who has 1 wants 2.

He who has 5 wants 10.

He who has 20 wants 40.

He who has 50 wants 100.

We all want more, and more, and more, and much more.

The Bible offers this wise perspective on gratitude: "Not that I speak in respect of want: for I have learned, in whatsoever state I am, therewith to be content.[29]

---

28 Alberto Castillo, "Todos Queremos Más," Genius, accessed March 15, 2021, https://genius.com/Alberto-castillo-todos-queremos-mas-lyrics.

29 "Philippians 4:11," KJV, https://www.kingjamesbibleonline.org/Philippians-4-11/.

How can the value of gratitude help create delta in your life? While the answer may be simple, it may be hard to implement. Try these three steps:

1. Focus on what you have, instead of what you don't.

2. Express gratitude often for it.

3. Be content.

Vocalizing Gratitude

Early one Monday morning, a professor asked his students if they had had a good weekend. One young student complained that his weekend had been horrible because he had his wisdom teeth extracted. Then the student asked the professor, "Why are you always so cheerful?"

> "I don't have to chase extraordinary moments to find happiness—it's right in front of me if I'm paying attention and practicing gratitude."
>
> – Brené Brown as told to Gretchen Rubin, *Forbes*, July 15, 2011

The professor shared a lesson he learned years before: "Every morning when I get up, I have a choice. I can decide how I want to approach life that day. Every morning, I choose to be cheerful."

He then recounted how his morning had gone. His car broke down and he had to walk to class. That could have ruined the day, but he felt lucky since his car could have broken down anywhere along the 17 miles to work, but it stalled just off the freeway, within walking distance to campus. He was able to get to work, call roadside assistance, and teach his class.

"If my car was meant to break down today, it couldn't have been arranged in a more convenient fashion," he shared with his class.[30]

Embracing the value of gratitude makes it a part of you. One of the fruits of focusing on the value of gratitude is joy. When you express gratitude regularly, it positively affects your journey through life.

My Best Day

When friends or family ask my father, George, how he is doing, he happily declares, "This is my best day so far."

My father tells how he came to embrace this upbeat response:

A friend once greeted me by asking the age-old question, "How are you?"

Without hesitating, I replied, "Nearly perfect."

Seeming somewhat surprised, my friend good naturedly asked, "Oh, really! Just what is it, George, that is keeping you from being completely perfect?"

With a smile, I replied, "I still lie." We had a good laugh together.

In our society, the most frequently asked question, by a large margin, is, "How are you?" Or more expertly and warmly asked, "How ya doin'?"

The quick and common answer is the all-encompassing word, "Fine."

"Fine" is possibly the most non-creative, non-descriptive, ungrateful, blah answer ever devised.

---

30 Lee Ryan Miller, *Teaching Amidst the Neon Palm Trees* (Bloomington: 1stBooks, 2004).

Feeling as I do about the word fine, I have for years searched for a better answer. For a time, when asked "How ya doin'?" I experimented with the answer "Champion!"

When that lost its appeal, I switched to "Superb." When that began to sound hollow, I changed to "Not half bad," which came from my British friends. But my thirst for just the right answer was never quenched.

Then one day when I was feeling so full of joy that I could scarcely contain it, someone asked me, "How are you?" And without even thinking I blurted out, "This is my best day so far!" As I continued on my way, it suddenly occurred to me that I had finally found the answer I had been seeking for so long. That's how I felt in that moment and that's how I want to feel every day.

I love my dad's grateful nature. He is a pleasure to be around because his attitude of gratitude is comfortably contagious. I have seen the V Effect in action as his simple response of contentment and gratitude influences others to see the good in each and every day. The ripples spread to one friend, then two friends and beyond.

Gratitude Grade

Here are a few ideas to help you make delta with the things you value as you shine a spotlight on the value of gratitude in your personal and professional life.

Gratitude Tools

To add to or enhance the value of gratitude:

1. Establish the habit of keeping a gratitude journal. At the end of the day, take time to note two or three things you are grateful for that day.

2. Write a "thank you" note to someone who recently helped you.

3. Recognize gratitude, express it, live it. William Arthur Ward wrote, "God gave you a gift of 86,400 seconds today. Have you used one to say 'thank you?'"[31]

4. Jot down a few notes about a person you consider to be grateful. What do they do to give this impression? How can you emulate what you see in this person?

> "Gratitude is the healthiest of all human emotions. The more you express gratitude for what you have, the more likely you will have even more to express gratitude for."
>
> – Zig Ziglar as told to Tom Ziglar, "The Gratitude Journey"

A former employee, Catherine Smith, sent me the following email in 2014. The subject line simply read "Thanks."

Last week a former resident emailed me concerning some problems with the new apartment manager and asked if I could help. He gave me some kind compliments and I felt those were derived from you. Thank you for teaching me how to be a good employee. Thank you for caring about others more than yourself. You showed me how to care for the people who lived there as well as caring for your interests; you taught me those don't have to be different.... The people who loved living at your apartment complex gave me credit for helping them feel cared for, but I couldn't have done that if you hadn't cared about them first. I feel blessed that I know you and have the opportunity to work for you.

Gratefully,
Catherine

---

31 William Arthur Ward, Goodreads, https://www.goodreads.com/quotes/101344-god-gave-you-a-gift-of-86-400-seconds-today.

Catherine's gratitude was simple, but her sincere expression has stayed with me for years. Thank you, Catherine, for taking a few of your 86,400 daily seconds to express gratitude!

This is how the value of gratitude is put into practice. Catherine's note inspired me to write similar notes of gratitude to spread the impact of the V Effect.

Who in your life can you lift with a thank-you note? Who might treasure your words of thanks? How can you extend the ripples of a grateful persona?

Here are a few related values from Appendix 1:

- Adaptability
- Appreciation
- Contentment
- Devotion
- Generosity
- Liberty
- Positivity
- Satisfaction
- Thankfulness

4. The Value of Service: Con Gusto

Jack McConnell was one of seven children born to a Methodist minister father and a stay-at-home mother. Jack's parents had to be careful with money. While the McConnell family did not enjoy financial wealth, they were spiritually wealthy and eager to share *that* wealth with others.

Jack remembers that his family ate dinner together every night. Each time they gathered around the table his father looked into the eyes of his children and asked, "What did you do for someone today?"[32] They all knew their father wanted an answer, so they prepared by performing acts of service that they could report back with confidence to their father. Every evening each child shared what he or she did and who they had helped.

---

32 "And What Did You Do for Someone Today?" Newsweek, June 18, 2001, https://www.newsweek.com/and-what-did-you-do-someone-today-153707.

Young Jack became Jack McConnell, M.D., who directed the development of the tuberculosis tine test. He helped develop the polio vaccine, oversaw the formulation of Tylenol, and was a member of the group that created the MRI machine. Dr. McConnell also founded Volunteers in Medicine, a group which helps retired members of the medical profession serve and volunteer at free clinics.

He gratefully acknowledged the legacy of service and selflessness his father instilled in him. He and his siblings continued to serve for the rest of their lives, their motivation unchanged. They wanted to be ready to confidently share their acts of service if asked, "And what did you do for someone today?"

Called to Serve

Few of us have cured the common cold or manufactured a pill to ease aches and pains, but many of us were raised in families dedicated to service. When I was young I wanted to serve as a missionary for my church. One of my motivations was to emulate the examples set for me. My older brother and my parents served missions in their youth, and I wanted to follow their examples.

As the time to serve as a missionary grew closer, I had become a skilled college basketball player. I was no longer asked "when" I would serve, but "if." It was a legitimate question.

No one in my faith is required to serve a two-year mission. Excelling in my sport could be my mission. I began to doubt my original goal. I knew I could be an athlete and represent my faith and my school and inspire young people through sport. Others had done that admirably. I struggled with the decision. Choosing to serve a mission, or making any serious religious commitment, is a very private and personal matter. My main fear was that serving God as a missionary for two years would mean the end of my basketball playing days, a sport I loved and did not want to give up. I spoke with one of my faith leaders, sharing all of my concerns with him.

He listened attentively, then told me if I would diligently serve a mission, I would return and become a better basketball player than I was then.

His words were comforting but hard to believe. How could I take a two-year break from playing basketball and return to my team at Brigham Young University, two years older and actually be a better player? It didn't add up for me.

Finally, after much prayer, I decided to go. I acknowledged that I had been blessed—so very blessed—for 19 years of my life. A full-time mission would allow me to forget about myself and serve others by giving my time and heart to them. If that meant basketball was over for me and I needed to move on to other things, I came to the conclusion I could accept that.

Once I made up my mind, I had to tell my coach. That wasn't easy. He was upset. He felt that my leaving would disrupt the cohesiveness of the team. He did not have anyone to fill my position, and he told me when I returned I would not immediately step back into my starting position. I'd have to earn the spot.

I didn't want to disappoint my coach. He had given me many opportunities. So, I decided to postpone my missionary service and spend another year playing basketball at BYU in order to give him a year to recruit and fill my position on the team.

I enjoyed competing during my sophomore year. The team had a solid roster made up of Danny Ainge, Fred Roberts, and Greg Kite (all future NBA players), other excellent players, and me. The next year Danny Ainge led the BYU team to victory over Notre Dame and into the Elite Eight during March Madness of 1981.[33]

I wasn't missed.

---

33 "BYU vs. Notre Dame: 1981 Sweet 16 | FULL GAME," March Madness, YouTube video, March 19, 2020, https://www.youtube.com/watch?v=V-Zmq9qcH7Q.

I remember the thrill of opening my missionary call and being assigned to serve in the Madrid, Spain, area. It was time to set basketball aside. I decided not to shoot a single jump shot while I was there, but I ran and exercised whenever I had the opportunity, usually once a week. I knocked on a lot of doors and climbed a lot of apartment building stairs; the stairs helped keep me in shape. I also had an early morning dunking drill where I would dunk a ball on a net-less (most of the time) rim while my missionary companions tried to catch it before it hit the ground (thank you, companions!) so we wouldn't disturb our neighbors with the "thump-thump-thump" of the ball. I wanted to enjoy the full promise made by my church leader. I wanted to make his words prophetic: "You will become a better basketball player." I was striving to be a diligent missionary, but I maintained my dream of returning to play college basketball.

We all are given various opportunities to choose how we can best serve others. There are many ways, large and small, to do it. The point is that we take action and serve. As we give of ourselves to lift another, the rewards always seem to land back in our lap.

Con Gusto

There is always work to be done for those who serve and volunteer their time and talents. How do you respond when asked to help? I learned a wonderful way to respond to service requests from a sister missionary I had the privilege of working closely with in Spain. She was different from most. Whenever she was asked to do something, she answered, "Con gusto!" Which translates to "With pleasure!" She was occasionally teased for her excitement and her predictability. At times, we mimicked her, declaring, "Con gusto" when asked to serve. But what started off with friendly teasing evolved to admiration and respect as we began to recognize the lesson she was teaching us. She happily served in any way she could. She lived to serve with pleasure and became a model of loving service. She served "con gusto." We followed her lead and were better for it. It felt good to be able to say with sincerity, "Con gusto," when asked to help in any way. The V Effect of her example was long-lasting in the lives of many people and it lives on in my life 40 years later.

The Little Things Matter

Some examples of service are subtle and often overlooked. During a football game in the fall of 2016, Dak Prescott, quarterback for the Dallas Cowboys, finished drinking water from a paper cup and tried to toss the cup over his shoulder and into the trash. Blame it on a tired arm late in the game, or blame it on a bad angle, but the cup missed the garbage can. Instead of leaving it for someone else to pick up, Prescott stood up, walked over, picked up the paper cup, and dropped it in the trash can.

What Prescott did not realize was that the entire eight-second act was caught by a television camera. In a world where loud and arrogant athletes often appear to be the norm, here was the team leader stopping to pick up his own trash.

> "What we do for ourselves dies with us. What we do for others and the world remains and is immortal."
>
> – Albert Pike, *Morals and Dogma of the Ancient and Accepted Scottish Rite of Freemasonry*

Sports commentator Colin Cowherd talked about Prescott on his show soon after the incident saying, "The little things matter. It doesn't look like much, but it mattered to Dak Prescott. 'Cause the little things always become big things.' Conscientious is Dak Prescott. Aware. Concerned about those around him.... Little stuff.

Now you're going to say to yourself, Colin, this is ridiculous.... That Dak Prescott on the bench, toss over his shoulder, just because that cup didn't go in the garbage can, we all know somebody else is going to clean it up. But it bothered Dak Prescott enough to walk over and put that little paper cup in the big garbage can. It bothered him enough. That's a guy who's going to give you extra reps at practice; who's going to open a door for a teammate; who's going to make sure that everybody is included in the huddle. All that little stuff becomes big stuff."[34]

I agree with everything Mr. Cowherd said, and I'm now a big fan of Dak Prescott.

Business cultures that embrace the value of Dak Prescott–type small and simple service receive the financial delta of happy and returning customers. Particularly in a connected world where one bad experience can lead to a lasting online review, quality service matters.

Ritz-Carlton Service

I've always enjoyed hearing stories of the exceptional service offered by the Ritz-Carlton hotel chain.[35] The following is a story I read a while back that has remained with me. The events took place at the Ritz-Carlton, Beijing. I hope it sticks with you as it has with me.

A couple from the United States traveled to Beijing with their first child, a six-month-old baby girl. They were nervous about traveling with her on the 16-hour flight to China.

---

34 "Dak Prescott Impressed Colin Cowherd by Picking up After Himself," The Herd with Colin Cowherd, YouTube video, November 21, 2016, https://www.youtube.com/watch?v=cZOPyoMY-SYI.

35 "Let Us Stay with You," The Ritz-Carlton, https://www.ritzcarlton.com/en/let-us-stay-with-you.

Before the flight, they had inquired about babysitting services at the hotel where they would be staying. When they arrived at the hotel, they received a warm welcome from the staff that put them at ease. They were then escorted to their room. Hotel management supplied a baby tub with rubber ducks, a bottle steamer, milk warmer, and a night-light. They were also pleased to find a humidifier to offer relief from the dry air that is common in Beijing. The family was overwhelmed by the hotel staff's attention to detail.

Sadly, the baby soon developed a rash on her neck and body. The babysitter/room attendant took the initiative, on her day off, to find out the hours of a pediatric hospital nearby. She knew it would be challenging to get an appointment on a weekday with no notice and learned that if the couple wanted to see a doctor, they would have to wait in line. At 2:00 a.m. the babysitter went to the hospital to obtain a number and a place in line for the guests. Then she waited in line for more than six hours. When the hotel guests arrived at the hospital, they waited 15 minutes to see the pediatrician. The parents were in tears and very touched by the babysitter's efforts. Upon departure, they noted that this was their first Ritz-Carlton experience, but definitely not their last.

> "Doing nothing for others is the undoing of ourselves."
> – Horace Mann in *Thoughts by Jessie K. Freeman and Sarah S. B. Yule*

Imagine the V Effect that occured as this couple shared their Ritz-Carlton experience with others.

A Million Dollar Lesson

Business consultant Petey Parker shared what he called, "A Million

Dollar Lesson." He flew to Dallas to meet with a client. As he exited the airport, a cab pulled up.

"The driver rushed to open the passenger door for me and made sure I was comfortably seated before he closed the door. As he got in the driver's seat, he mentioned that the neatly folded Wall Street Journal next to me was for my use. He then asked me what type of music I would enjoy."

Parker was stunned by the level of service and asked the driver about his story. The driver said he used to work in the corporate world, but that it wore him down. Instead, he wanted to find his niche, something that would bring him pride and allow him to help others.

"I knew I would never be a rocket scientist, but I love driving cars, being of service, and feeling like I have done a full day's work and done it well. I evaluated my personal assets and…wham! I became a cab driver.

"One thing I know for sure, to be good in my business I could simply just meet the expectations of my passengers. But to be GREAT in my business, I have to EXCEED the customer's expectations! I like both the sound and the return of being 'great' better than just getting by on 'average.'"[36]

We can be good at service or we can strive to exceed our customer's expectations and provide great service. It's in our hands.

The Cab Ride

Speaking of cab drivers, author Kent Nerburn used to drive a cab for a living. He shared how one simple ride changed how he looks at life and its small moments of service. He wrote:

---

36 Petey Parker, "A Million Dollar Lesson," Inspire21, September 14, 2011, https://inspire21.com/?s=million+dollar+lesson.

Twenty years ago, I drove a cab for a living. One time I arrived in the middle of the night for a pickup at a building that was dark except for a single light in a ground floor window.

Under these circumstances, many drivers would just honk once or twice, wait a minute, then drive away. But I had seen too many impoverished people who depended on taxis as their only means of transportation. Unless a situation smelled of danger, I always went to the door. This passenger might be someone who needs my assistance, I reasoned to myself. So, I walked to the door and knocked.

> From my fortune cookie:
>
> "Life's greatest privilege is being able to help someone in need."

"Just a minute," answered a frail, elderly voice.

Nerburn then describes the woman who answers the door. She was in her 80s and she was dressed like a woman out of a 1940's movie. By her side was a nylon suitcase. Nerburn took the suitcase to the cab, then returned to assist the woman.

He continues the story:

She took my arm and we walked slowly toward the curb. She kept thanking me for my kindness. "It's nothing," I told her. "I just try to treat my passengers the way I would want my mother treated." "Oh, you're such a good boy," she said. When we got in the cab, she gave me an address, then asked, "Could you drive through downtown?"

"It's not the shortest way," I answered quickly.

"Oh, I don't mind," she said. "I'm in no hurry. I'm on my way to a hospice."

I looked in the rear-view mirror. Her eyes were glistening.

"I don't have any family left," she continued. "The doctor says I don't have very long."

I quietly reached over and shut off the meter. "What route would you like me to take?" I asked.

Nerburn then recounts how the two of them drove for two hours through the city and how his passenger showed him the building where she had once worked as an elevator operator. They also drove through the neighborhood where she and her husband had lived when they were newlyweds. They drove past other personal landmarks and occasionally stopped for a time as the woman stared silently. As the sun began to rise, the woman told him she was tired and it was time to go. He then drove to the address she had given him. They arrived at a small convalescent home. Two orderlies came out to the cab as soon as they pulled up. Nerburn opened the trunk and took the suitcase to the door. The woman was helped to a wheelchair.

Nerburn concludes the story with this exchange:

"How much do I owe you?" she asked, reaching into her purse.

"Nothing," I said.

"You have to make a living," she answered.

"There are other passengers."

Almost without thinking, I bent and gave her a hug. She held onto me tightly.

"You gave an old woman a little moment of joy," she said. "Thank you."

I squeezed her hand, then walked into the dim morning light. Behind me, a door shut. It was the sound of the closing of a life.

Nerburn then summarizes his thoughts on the experience:

I didn't pick up any more passengers that shift. I drove aimlessly, lost in thought. For the rest of that day, I could hardly talk. What if that woman had gotten an angry driver, or one who was impatient to end his shift? What if I had refused to take the run, or had honked once, then driven away?

On a quick review, I don't think that I have done anything more important in my life. We're conditioned to think that our lives revolve around great moments. But great moments often catch us unaware—beautifully wrapped in what others may consider a small one.[37]

Keep your eyes open for the next cab ride to heaven and other opportunities to serve. You never know when they might appear and when they do, be ready to act – Con Gusto!

Cascade Endodontics

I was recently the beneficiary of remarkable and unforgettable service.

I awoke one morning with a sharp tooth pain. I called my endodontist's office at 6:34 a.m., knowing I would get the voicemail recording. I left a message hoping a receptionist would call back once the office opened. At 6:39 a.m. Dr. Jon Jensen, my endodontist, personally

37 Kent Nerburn, Make Me an Instrument of your Peace (New York: Harper Collins, 2010). www.kentnerburn.com.

called me back. He asked a couple of questions and then said, "Can you be to my office by 7:30 a.m.?" I excitedly responded, "Yes!"

As soon as I entered the office door, Dr. Jensen's assistant shuffled me to the X-ray machine. Dr. Jensen then studied the X-ray and discovered an abscessed tooth that needed a root canal. He went to work, aided by his skilled assistant, and soon my pain subsided. I walked out of his office at 8:15 a.m. with a smile on my face, grateful for his concern and service. I never tire of telling this story of Dr. Jensen's responsiveness, selflessness, and professionalism—values we should all consider adding to our Priority Values list.

Service Grade

Are you naturally service-oriented? What grade do you give yourself? The following ideas may help you improve your service grade and create meaningful delta.

Service Tools

1. What "little stuff" can you do? If you were to choose to include the value of service on your My Priority Values list and correspondingly to your life, how would you start? Quiet your mind and let the ideas flow. Write them down. Then form a plan to act on those ideas.

2. Start small and start local. There is much need in the world, and in our own communities. Where would you like to start your service? Where can you make a dent in your neighborhood, office, or city? Often the greatest service we render is in our own sphere, not in far reaching places. What do your children need? Your spouse or partner? Your coworker? Do you have a child who is behind on their schoolwork who could use a little extra help?

I recently met a retired grandmother who looked for service opportunities with well-known organizations. In one such assignment, she helped children with their reading. It was fulfilling, but she soon realized her own grandchildren were struggling. She called her grandchildren's school, asked how she could help, and went to work.

If you're ready to expand beyond your own family, look to your neighborhood. There are so many ways to serve. A "good news report" on television highlighted a neighbor who picked up trash blown around after frequent windstorms in his area. He had the time, he was happy to do it, and his neighbors were grateful for his small acts of service.

If you're ready to move beyond your neighborhood, look to your city. Are there food pantries that need to be stocked? Are there meals for the elderly waiting to be delivered? What skills do you have that can be used to serve others? Or what collective skills could your organization offer?

I know of a man who went to law school and did well in his career, but he wanted more and knew he could give more. He went back to school, earned his English as a Second Language certificate, and now he helps the children of refugees acclimate and excel in a local school district.

What difference will you and/or your organization make by taking time to serve others—to do little stuff like Dak Prescott? You may become someone's role model. You may earn a loyal customer for life like my endodontist. Choose to serve and see what wonderful adventures lay ahead!

Here are a few more values from Appendix 1 that are similar to the value of service that you might consider adding to your list of Priority Values:

- Anticipation
- Cooperation
- Dependability
- Energy
- Work
- Helpfulness
- Joy
- Proactivity
- Selflessness
- Virtue

5. The Value of Integrity: Do What Is Right

If someone referred to me as a mama's boy, they would be spot on. I feel I had a magical connection with my mother. She passed away in 2011 and I miss her dearly. I can't remember a single moment where I was upset with my mom. If I had to describe her in one word, that word would be integrity. She was tough and organized and wise and loyal and faithful, but she would best be described as a woman of integrity. She never wavered from her values and principles. I never saw her contemplate compromising herself in any way. She was as solid as a rock. Integrity is one of my Priority Values because of her. I want to be like my mom.

When we are young and hear the word "integrity," we may understand that integrity has something to do with honesty. As we get older, we realize integrity is more than being honest. When the value of integrity is ingrained in one's character, there is no room for excuses, small fibs, lies, or other forms of dishonesty.

Out of Bounds

During a basketball game when I played in Spain, the ball was deflected out of bounds. The referee judged that the ball went out on the other team, and it was now my team's ball. One of my teammates took the ball out of bounds and prepared to throw it in.

That is when things got a little crazy. My teammate knew the referee made the wrong call, and that the ball should have gone to the other team. When the ball was thrown to him, he intentionally threw it out of bounds so the referee could make the correct call.

Four high school boys afflicted with spring fever skipped morning classes. After lunch they reported to the teacher that they had a flat tire.

Much to their relief she smiled and said, "Well, you missed a test today so take seats apart from one another and take out a piece of paper."

Still smiling, she waited for them to sit down. Then she said:

"First Question: Which tire was flat?"

I was surprised. I had never seen that happen before in a basketball game, but I quickly realized that my teammate had chosen to be fair. I respected him for how he handled the situation. No one would have condemned him had he done nothing to correct the error. He would have been justified to follow the referee's ruling, but it mattered to him to do the right thing. No matter the consequences.

Andy Roddick

During a tennis match in 2005, Andy Roddick was inches away from joining Andre Agassi in the quarterfinals of the Rome Masters. Roddick was leading 5-3 in the second set and had triple match point when his opponent, Fernando Verdasco, served a ball that the line judge called out. He could have let the call stand. Instead, Roddick overturned a double fault call—he knew it was in and declared Verdasco's serve an ace. Roddick ended up losing the match and the ability to move to the next round.

"I didn't think it was anything extraordinary. The umpire would have done the same thing if he had come down to the court and looked," Roddick said later. "I just saved him the trip. He's working hard up there."[38]

These examples of integrity in sports have stayed with me because I am amazed at how quickly and easily the players decided to do the right thing, no matter the situation. When we choose to exercise integrity on a case-by-case basis, the decision to do right is much harder.

Keep Your Agreement

Why do people lie? Why is it so easy to lie?

Here are a few reasons:

1. People lie to avoid consequences. We think the hurt of the lie is less painful than the consequences of telling the truth.

2. We lie to get out of things we don't want to do. Professors all across the world can attest to the fact that a surprising number of students' grandparents die during finals week.

---

38 Associated Press, "Roddick upset by Verdasco," ESPN, May 5, 2005, https://www.espn.com/sports/tennis/news/story?id=2053672.

3. We lie to create a new reality for ourselves. When our lives and our stories become mundane, it's easier to embellish a little, stretch the truth a little—to lie a little.

Lies may help get us out of a jam, but there are consequences when we compromise with the value of integrity.

Consider the story of a young man who went to a trusted leader, Nathan Eldon Tanner, to ask for advice. Tanner wrote of the experience:

> The young man said, "I made an agreement with a man that requires me to make certain payments each year. I am in arrears, and I can't make those payments, for if I do, it is going to cause me to lose my home. What shall I do?"
>
> I looked at him and said, "Keep your agreement."
>
> "Even if it costs me my home?"
>
> I said, "I am not talking about your home. I am talking about your agreement; and I think your wife would rather have a husband who would keep his word, meet his obligations, keep his pledges or his covenants, and have to rent a home than to have a home with a husband who will not keep his covenants and his pledges."[39]

Don't Do It!

Thousands of years ago a young man was celebrated for his integrity. His name was Joseph. He had a lot of brothers who were older, bigger, and stronger, however his lowly place down the family tree did not equate to humble behavior.

---

39 N. Eldon Tanner, "Keep Your Covenants," The Improvement Era, December 1966, 1136–1137, https://archive.org/details/improvementera6912unse/page/n81/mode/2up.

And Joseph dreamed a dream, and he told it to his brethren: and they hated him yet the more. And he said unto them, Hear, I pray you, this dream which I have dreamed: For behold, we were binding sheaves in the field, and, lo, my sheaf arose, and also stood upright; and, behold, your sheaves stood round about, and made obeisance to my sheaf. And his brethren said to him, Shalt thou indeed reign over us? Or shalt thou indeed have dominion over us? And they hated him yet the more for his dreams, and for his words. And he dreamed yet another dream, and told it his brethren, and said, Behold, I have dreamed a dream more; and behold, the sun and the moon and the eleven stars made obeisance to me.[40]

At this point Joseph's father had become annoyed and rebuked Joseph, and asked,

What is this dream that thou has dreamed? Shall I and thy mother and thy brethren indeed come to bow down ourselves to thee to the earth?[41]

His brothers had had enough of their arrogant little brother. When an opportunity came, they tossed him into a pit, ate a snack, waited for merchants to pass by, and sold Joseph for twenty pieces of silver. Joseph was sold again and ended up in Potiphar's house, Pharaoh's own Captain of the Guard.[42]

Potiphar came to love Joseph. Perhaps he loved him for his integrity as much as for the fact that Joseph brought him good luck. The Bible tells us:

---

40 "Genesis, 37:5–9," KJV, https://www.kingjamesbibleonline.org/Genesis-Chapter-37/#5.

41 "Genesis, 37:10," Ibid.

42 "Genesis, 37:24–36," Ibid.

And his master saw that the Lord was with him, and that the Lord made all that he did to prosper in his land.[43]

Joseph was promoted to overseer of Potiphar's house. Things were looking up until he was betrayed again. He had attracted the attention of Potiphar's wife. When she requested that Joseph lay with her, Joseph refused.[44]

> My master wotteth not what is with me in the house, and he hath committed all that he hath to my hand. There is none greater in this house than I; neither hath he kept back anything from me but thee, because thou art his wife: how then can I do this great wickedness, and sin against God?"[45]

We may not know her name, but we do know that Potiphar's wife was persistent. The Bible tells us that "day by day" she made the same request and he continually refused. Then she cornered him, and he fled from her, leaving behind his garment in her hand in his haste.[46]

That garment was enough for Mrs. Potiphar to frame Joseph for attempted rape, and she brought the garment forward.

> And she spake unto him according to these words, saying, The Hebrew servant, which thou hast brought unto us, came in unto me to mock me: And it came to pass, as I lifted my voice and cried, that he left his garment with me, and fled out. And it came to pass, when his master heard the words of his wife, which she spake unto him, saying, after this manner did thy servant to me; that his wrath was kindled. And Joseph's master took him, and

---

43 "Genesis, 39:3," Ibid.

44 "Genesis, 39:5–7," Ibid.

45 "Genesis, 39:8-9," Ibid.

46 "Genesis, 39:10–12," Ibid.

put him into the prison, a place where the king's prisoners were bound: and he was there in the prison.[47]

Thankfully, that was not the end of Joseph's story. After an additional series of events, Joseph comes out on top.

Striving for integrity delta does not lead to automatic happiness, though Joseph's personal story ended well. Joseph lived his life in harmony with his values in both good and bad times. He refused to do otherwise, no matter the consequences.

> "We need more integrity in *government.*
>
> ... We need men and women of courage and honest convictions, who will stand always ready to be counted for their integrity and not compromise for expediency, lust for power, or greed; and we need a people who will appreciate and support representatives of this caliber."
>
> – Nathan Eldon Tanner, "Integrity"

Do You Know Him?

I had an opportunity years ago to do business with a man well known in the local real estate market.

Before we entered into a negotiation, I asked my brother, who is the chief justice of the Utah Supreme Court, "Do you know this man?"

"Yes," he said. "When I worked as an attorney, I helped him through a tough legal battle. I like him. He's honest. He had multiple opportunities to modify the truth in the transaction and strengthen his position, and he refused to do it."

---

47 "Genesis, 39:17–20," Ibid.

I went forward with the transaction because of the validation my brother provided.

Every business or private deal offers opportunities to cheat, to be dishonest, to fudge. We have to police ourselves and must not base our morality on someone else's values. To do so may be like riding a sliding scale that only leads downward. Never let someone else's lack of moral values pull you into their sewer.

It's Not Enough to Be Fair

Several years ago, my friend, Tad Callister, and his business partner realized they needed to terminate an employee. Together they drafted a settlement to compensate the employee for his services. Tad thought the settlement was more than fair, but was still troubled, and stated:

> That night I felt a gloom come over me. I tried to dispel it by reasoning within myself that I had been fair, but the feeling would not leave. Then this impression came: "It's not enough to be fair; you must also strive to be Christlike." Adherence to the highest moral code is a hallmark of a woman or a man of integrity.[48]

Imagine the V Effect of striving to not only be fair, but to be Christlike.

President Abraham Lincoln suggested: let us live in accord with "the better angels of our nature."[49]

Are you living in accord with the better angels of your nature? How do you perceive how others speak of you? Would you be pleased or

---

48 Tad R. Callister, "Becoming Men and Women of Integrity," Brigham Young University (BYU) Speeches, December 6, 2011, https://speeches.byu.edu/talks/tad-r-callister/becoming-men-and-women-of-integrity/.

49 "First Inaugural Address of Abraham Lincoln," March 4, 1861, The Avalon Project, https://avalon.law.yale.edu/19th_century/lincoln1.asp.

devastated by their estimation of you? How you embrace the value of integrity may determine the tone of their conversation.

Integrity Is Forever

Amy Rees Anderson, a contributor to *Forbes*, wrote that if she could teach only one value to live by it would be integrity.

> Integrity is forever. Integrity means doing the right thing at all times and in all circumstances, whether or not anyone is watching. It takes having the courage to do the right thing, no matter what the consequences will be. Building a reputation of integrity takes years, but it takes only a second to lose it, so never allow yourself to ever do anything that would damage your integrity.

> "To thine own self be true,
> And it must follow, as the night the day,
> Thou canst not then be false to any man."
> —William Shakespeare, *Hamlet*, Act 1, Scene 3

Anderson goes on to outline how integrity and trust go hand in hand—how damaging it can be to lose trust and how valuable it is to be trusted in all circles.

> That person has lost their ability to be trusted as a person of integrity, which is the most valuable quality anyone can have in their life. Profit in dollars or power is temporary, but profit in a network of people who trust you as a person of integrity is forever.

Anderson closes with this powerful thought:

> Yes, the value of the trust others have in you goes beyond anything that can be measured because it brings along with it limitless opportunities and endless possibilities.... There is a plaque on

the wall of my office which reads, "Do what is right, let the consequence follow." It serves as a daily reminder that success will indeed come and go, but integrity is forever.[50]

Thank you, Amy Rees Anderson. Your words of wisdom on the value of integrity stand strong and forever.

Integrity Grade

What is your integrity quotient? What grade do you give yourself? The following may help you improve your integrity delta and that of your organization.

Integrity Tools

Integrity is such an important character trait that choosing to become a person of integrity—choosing to focus on the value of integrity—may be one of the best decisions you ever make.

How can you add to your integrity delta?

1. **Make decisions ahead of time.** When the sun is out, when the clouds are far away, decide to embrace integrity. When the storms hit, you will not wonder how to act. You'll know. The decision and the choice have already been made.

2. **Keep all promises, large and small.** Start small and keep going! If you promise to help a colleague, remember to do it! If you promise your daughter you'll watch her play softball, be there! If you have a deadline, keep it! No excuses.

3. **Don't compromise your standards.** There is an old saying that the end justifies the means. If you want to live the value

---

50 Amy Rees Anderson, "Success Will Come and Go, But Integrity Is Forever," Forbes, November 28, 2012, https://www.forbes.com/sites/amyanderson/2012/11/28/success-will-come-and-go-but-integrity-is-forever/?sh=ad697c3470f9.

of integrity, don't fall into that trap. Be transparent with your integrity.

Let me finish this chapter with a brief story. I bought landscaping bricks to improve a property, and after I left the store and arrived back at the property, I realized I had miscounted and underpaid. The mistake was small, less than $5, and could have easily been dismissed, but I returned to the store in order to pay the difference.

The clerk looked at me and said, "Thank you for being honest."

It was a small and simple thing, but I was surprised how good I felt when she said that to me. Having her verbally recognize that I was acting with integrity put a smile on my face and warmed my heart. Yes, it feels good to do the right thing when a few hundred pennies are involved. I am committed to act the same way if thousands of dollars are involved. I know that's how my mom would want it.

The following values from Appendix 1 include elements of the value of integrity:

- Accountability
- Consistency
- Courage
- Credibility
- Discipline
- Ethics
- Fidelity
- Honesty
- Honor
- Trust

6. The Value of Communication: I'm Going to Throw Up

Before the advent of the cell phone, private conversations with friends meant using the home phone with the longest cord.

Today, you can call, text, Skype, instant message, FaceTime, Zoom, Duo—the opportunities to connect are only limited by our contract or our Internet connection.

With all these resources, somehow, our society has regressed in its ability to effectively communicate. How odd it is that with all the progress we have made in modes of communication, we have digressed in our ability to connect with others in meaningful ways. How can we change course and swim against the growing tides of miscommunication and disconnection?

I continue to be reminded of the value of clear communication. I've experienced the pain of failed communication too often.

Shoveling in a Snowstorm

My niece worked years ago as one of my office managers. She was a terrific employee, dedicated to the job. She broke the negative assumption that hiring family is rarely a good idea.

One winter, our city was hit by a heavy snowstorm. When I checked on the property where my niece worked, I saw her shoveling the walks and making them safe for the residents. I was so impressed by her diligence and sacrifice as she struggled in the horrible weather, I said to her, "No one shovels snow in weather like this!"

One little sentence.

Thinking about it now, I recognize my comment could be taken multiple ways. She could have thought I was telling her she was dumb—"*No one* shovels snow in weather like this!" or I was telling her that she was amazing—"No one shovels snow in weather like *this!*"

I meant it as a compliment, but she heard criticism. And boy, was I in trouble. She went home and told her mother (my sister-in-law) who told my mother-in-law. You can imagine how popular I was in the days to come. In fact, it took some time to clear up the misunderstanding.

I learned a hard lesson, loud and clear. Communicate clearly. In fact, communicate so clearly that there can be no room for misunderstanding! Tone of voice, inflection, a smile, body language, eye contact, and gestures, all color how communication is received.

It's hard and takes effort. You know what you intend to communicate, and you think you communicate it perfectly—only to find out something went horribly wrong in the translation.

Throw Up

One spring my family all came down with the flu. It was awful—lots of vomiting. The kids were little at the time and often didn't make it to the bathroom in a timely fashion.

My four-year-old daughter, Laura, hesitantly said, "I'm going to throw up." Julie excitedly said, "Get in the bathroom and stand over the toilet."

"Why?" she asked.

"Because I don't want to clean up your mess here in the living room!" Julie answered.

Obediently, Laura rushed into the bathroom. Within seconds we all heard the splash of vomit hitting the floor.

> "The great enemy of communication is the illusion of it."
> —William Hollingsworth Whyte, "Is Anybody Listening?"
> *Fortune*, September 1950

Head bowed in defeat; Julie went to the bathroom to see what had happened. She found Laura, standing over the toilet, throwing up on the closed toilet lid and onto the floor.

Laura followed her mother's instructions explicitly, but her mother didn't tell her to lift the lid first. The results were not what her mother had hoped for.

Build Your Network

Let's take a minute and discuss a slightly different aspect of communication. What do you do when you walk into a room where there are 20-40 people? Do you size up the room and quickly decide who is a friend or foe?

- What will change if you enter a room and do not immediately seek out a comfortable friend?

- What will change if you enter a room and assume everyone there wants to talk with you and get to know you better?

- What will change if you enter a room assuming you will like everyone, and they will like you?

It is easy for me to meet new people. I'm usually confident starting a conversation. I have found value in being optimistic as I meet people for the first time and develop new relationships.

The following strategies have helped me to improve communication and increase networking success:

- Open your mouth. Begin the conversation.

- Introduce yourself.

- Talk to people in person.

- Give people the opportunity to look you in the eye.

- Show an interest in the conversation.

- Seek opportunities to build new relationships.

"Hello, I'm Devin Durrant," I'll say. "I'd like to get to know you better." This is the start I've made on multiple occasions. When you are ready to move into a new career, or seize a new opportunity, you begin by opening your mouth. When you meet someone who is in the same industry as you, take time to develop a relationship. Show an interest in them and what they do. The importance of opening the lines of communication with people of common interests is immeasurable.

It's not too difficult. Most people like to talk about what they do, how they became successful, or the assets they own. Most people will open up to you and be more than happy to talk about themselves. The next step is to stay in touch—keep checking in.

> "If you want one year of prosperity, grow grain. If you want 10 years of prosperity, grow trees. If you want 100 years of prosperity, grow people."
>
> – Chinese Proverb

Keep talking. At first people were nice to me because I am Devin Durrant, the basketball player. But there were many people who had no clue who I am and treated me kindly simply because there are a lot of decent people in the world.

Networking means getting to know people in your industry or profession; people trying to do the same thing you are doing. Early in my professional career, I decided to make as many friends as I could who shared my professional interests. I was not shy. I let people know what I was doing, what I was looking for, and how I needed help.

Make Friends

When I was first involved in real estate investing, I decided to get a real estate license. I believed the license would provide valuable knowledge, experience, and commission savings, although I didn't plan to become a real estate agent. I wanted to be an investor.

My plan backfired when I began discussing possible investments with friends and associates. Some of them stopped talking to me. They anticipated that I was trying to take part of their commission. Then, conversations shut down entirely. I was shocked and unprepared for that response, so I chose to deactivate my real estate license. What mattered were the people, not the paper. Networking, relationships, and communication was what I wanted. I hoped people in my line of work would communicate with me. I wanted them to see me as an ally and friend.

I periodically receive emails listing real estate deals from a Realtor in a nearby county. One property looked interesting, so I set up a time to visit the property and meet the Realtor.

My plans changed and I decided to pass on the property. I quickly contacted the Realtor. The drive to the property was 30-40 minutes for him, and I did not want to waste his time. He appreciated my consideration.

Over the next few weeks, we got to know each other better and built a relationship, even though I passed on the initial offering. I asked if he had any properties closer to my home. He was planning to look at one that day. We walked through the property together. I liked it, and quickly closed on it with my son as my partner. The Realtor made the deal with us before he had sent the information to his investor pool. He might have made more money by contacting all his investors, but because we had opened the lines of communication and formed a friendship, he was willing to forego a greater profit.

The Sheepherder

Years ago, I met a gentleman named Sherm Hislop, a military man who was probably in his late 70s at the time. On his business card his title was "Sheepherder." He became my mentor. After his military career, he became a contractor and built several large apartment complexes near my home. He had been working in the housing market for some time and knew a lot of people.

Sherm was kind and willing to give me advice and direction. He had watched me play basketball years earlier and always had a basketball story to share when we visited in his office.

His counsel was valuable. Later he built an apartment complex for me.

Sherm introduced me to his son, Steve, who helped manage Sherm's properties. Steve phoned one day and said, "Devin, I know you're involved in this multi-family community. I've got a dilemma. Will you recommend the name of a Realtor who can list a property for me? I have friends who jointly own a property but can't agree how to liquidate the complex. Can you recommend a Realtor who can help them?"

"Sure," I said, "but first, why are they selling?" He told me they had owned this property for several years but lived in different cities. Over the course of time, they found one reason or another to dislike each other, and no longer wanted to be partners. They both wanted to sell and get their respective share of the proceeds.

I decided to look at the property myself, thanked Steve, then pledged to give him $10,000 if I bought the apartment complex—all because he thought to call me for help.

Steve arranged for separate meetings with each man. Over time we all agreed on a price. I bought the property, held it for 15 years, then sold it. I'll always be grateful to Sherm and Steve Hislop. They helped me create delta in quantitative and qualitative ways. Our relationship would not have happened if I had not knocked on their door, opened communication, and taken steps to build my network.

Communicate in Writing

Communication does not always need to be verbal. Notes, texts, and emails are effective ways to check in and keep conversations going. After an initial in-person meeting, I will follow up with a letter. If the purpose of my communication relates to the acquisition of a property, I will clearly lay out my research and proposal. If we are negotiating a price and are still far apart on the numbers, I explain the reasons behind my offered price in the letter and take the time to provide more information. When appropriate, I share comparable sales information and make a logical argument to support my offer price.

If you allow others the opportunity to consider your point of view by outlining it in a letter, the other party has time to understand, adjust, or compromise without the pressure of a face-to-face situation. If done correctly, writing provides clarity and reduces or eliminates misunderstandings.

Verbal Communication Skills

My most memorable college course was an English usage class recommended by my older brother and taught by Don Norton. The V Effect of his teachings has been impressive for me to witness. He taught me to be aware of how I speak and write, which has blessed my life in multiple ways, and yet it has also been a bit of a curse. At times, I correct the speech of others in my head when I should be listening. I have come to value proper speech and eloquent communication. It is high on the list of things I value. I know that improving speech is another way to create delta in both personal and professional communication.

Consider the following examples of how we might improve verbal communication.

1. We overuse filler words. "I mean…" is a prime example. Listen carefully to today's political pundits and you will be surprised at the frequency of use. Or listen to how your friends talk and you'll see what I mean—no pun intended. Other words and phrases that are overused include "you know," "um," and "uh."

2. How about this phrase: "Does that make sense?" I feel a bit insulted when someone asks me that question. It seems they think I'm not smart enough to listen and understand what they are saying. If you feel inclined to ask, "Does that make sense?" try speaking more clearly so you do make sense. Or you might seek confirmation of understanding in a different way.

3. We often start sentences with the phrase "The thing is…." I think we use this to get our foot in the conversation, but most of the time it is unnecessary.

> "Speak clearly, if you speak at all; carve every word before you let it fall."
>
> – Oliver Wendell Holmes, Sr., "A Rhymed Lesson (Urania),"
> *The Poetical Works of Oliver Wendell Holmes, Volume 2*

4. Like, like, like, like, like has become very ingrained in teens and young adults in recent years. Even adults overuse and misuse the word "like." Frequent use of "like" can be easily reduced.

5. Eliminating profanity is a simple way to elevate your speech. Profanity distracts from your message and will lower you in the eyes of a good portion of your audience.

6. Keep your communication civil. It's common to attack the messenger rather than the message. Even with our differences of opinion, we can still communicate in a respectful manner.

My oldest son interviewed for jobs with Intuit, Google, and Facebook. He was hired by all three companies at different times. Many people apply to work for these world-class companies, but few are hired. My son credits much of his success to his ability to speak eloquently and clearly during his job interviews and refrain from using the "filler words" of our day.

Civil Communication

Before moving on, let me add one addition to my earlier point of communicating civilly. One of the greatest minds ever, Benjamin Franklin, learned what he might change in himself to communicate more effectively. Consider this wisdom-filled personal example of how Franklin learned to temper his words and the four positive outcomes that resulted:

I made it a rule to forbear all direct contradiction to the sentiments of others, and all positive assertion of my own. I even forbid myself…the use of every word or expression in the language that imported a fix'd opinion, such as certainly, undoubtedly, etc., and I adopted, instead of them, I conceive, I apprehend, or I imagine a thing to be so or so; or it so appears to me at present. When another asserted something that I thought an error, I deny'd myself the pleasure of contradicting him abruptly, and of showing immediately some absurdity in his proposition; and in answering I began by observing that in certain cases or circumstances his opinion would be right, but in the present case there appear'd or seem'd to me some differences, etc. I soon found the advantage of this change in my manner; the conversations I engage'd in went on more pleasantly. The modest way in which I propos'd my opinions procur'd them a readier reception and less contradiction; I had less mortification when I was found to be in the wrong, and I more easily prevail'd with others to give up their mistakes and join with me when I happened to be in the right.[51]

I hope these words from a man who has impacted millions of lives over the course of many years have you thinking how you might become a delta maker by improving your communication skills.

Communication Grade

Where are you today with the value of communication? What changes can you make to improve your communication—your verbal skills? Your writing skills? Your networking ability? What grade do you give yourself? Here are a few more ideas that might help you improve your communication grade and make a positive difference personally and professionally.

Communication Tools

It is a fundamental truth (taught often by my father) that the only time your children (or spouse, or employee, etc.) can really talk to you is when you are with them. Due to the distractions that surround us, let me rephrase this truth. "The only time your children can really talk to you is when you are with them *and paying attention to them.*" In that spirit, I share the following story written by my father (and I do so with his permission):

The greatest victory I ever won was on our home court. My oldest son, Matt, was in the ninth grade. He wanted with all his heart to be an athlete. He was pretty good at basketball, but he wasn't growing much.

---

51 Benjamin Franklin, Benjamin Franklin's Autobiography: A Norton Critical Edition, ed. Joyce E. Chaplin (New York: W. W. Norton, 2012).

During that period of time he was pretty ornery. He would seldom talk to me, and when he did it was in an unpleasant tone. Yet I'd heard that over at the school he was the most friendly and amiable boy on campus.

I wanted him to talk to me because I felt that something was troubling him. My desires for such a conversation had not yet been rewarded. One day we were out playing basketball before dinner, just the two of us. We were playing a good game of one-on-one. I'd score and then he'd score. While we were playing, I started talking to him. I asked him, "How did it go in school today?" His only answer was uncomfortable silence. I raised my voice and asked, "Did you hear me? How did it go at school today?"

Finally, he answered, "Why do you ask such dumb questions?" A bit surprised at his abrupt reply, I thought to myself, "I guess that was a dumb question."

I decided to upgrade my queries. I asked, "What did you have for school lunch?" He replied, "What does that matter? Every day we have the same tasteless stuff."

I wasn't quite sure just what to ask him next. We shot a few more baskets. In my silence I was wishing he weren't so unhappy. Then an inspired question came to me. I asked, "How did it go in gym today?" His countenance brightened as he enthusiastically replied, "Hey, in gym today I did pretty good." He started talking to me. We bounced the ball a little less and just stood around between baskets. As our conversation thickened, he spoke with some emotion. "Dad, I don't know if you ever wonder why I'm so ornery."

I replied, "Oh, no. I never wonder about that."

"Well, the reason is that I don't like the way I look."

I was silent for a few seconds. Then I said, "You look good. You look just like me." With that he kind of gulped with a slight indication of pain.

"No, Dad, you look all right but I don't. I'm not as big as I want to be, and I wear glasses. When I look at myself in the mirror, I just don't look like an athlete."

I knew what he was talking about. As a youth, I'd had some of those same problems. He kept talking to me, and I didn't know what to say. I could have said, "Don't be silly. You look like an athlete. You'll grow one of these days so don't worry about it. You'll be a great athlete." But I didn't give those pat answers. I just listened, and I thought, and I cared.

Just then my wife, Marilyn, stepped outside and invited us to come to dinner. We left the basketball court and walked across the back lawn. As we passed under the big trees, I put my arm around his shoulder. We climbed up the back stairs. There was a feeling of love and understanding between us. I hadn't answered any of his questions, but he'd had a chance to tell me, his dad, how he felt and that had helped him.[52]

If you would like to change and improve your communication skills, take this story to heart. Consider how it might apply to your situation and those you need to communicate better with. Here are several more ideas on how to communicate more effectively:

1. **Find the desire.** My father knew something was wrong. He wasn't satisfied to let it go and hope for the best. He desired to communicate.

---

52 George Durrant, Scones for the Heart: 184 Morsels of Wit and Wisdom to Warm the Soul (Springville: Cedar Fort, 2001), 72–73.

2. **Pick a good time**. My father picked a moment when he was having a good time with Matt and the chance for a successful conversation was prime. We've all experienced times when high levels of stress made a harmless conversation harmful.

3. **Ask for help.** My father is a talented speaker and writer. He understands how to communicate. But even he admits, "An inspired question came to me." Don't hesitate to ask for help or inspiration.

4. **Listen and improve.** Communication is a two-way street. It's not truly communication if we talk without listening or lecture without allowing the other person to speak.

5. **Elevate your speech.** One way to elevate your speech is to listen to the words and phrases you use. Eliminate words and expressions that might make you appear less intelligent or immature.

6. **Don't expect perfection.** You don't have to give perfect answers to be helpful. Just offer the best of yourself as a friend and listener.

7. **Empathize**. If you've gone through a similar experience, share it. If you're struggling, sometimes it's a relief to know someone else has been in a similar situation and survived. Be careful not to minimize another's struggle as you outline your success during a time of trial.

I endorse the importance of the value of communication. Often, the root of our problems is some sort of miscommunication. I recognize that I need to communicate more clearly with those in my sphere of influence and am constantly striving to improve. Working on these ideas will create the delta you seek.

Here are 10 more values that include elements of communication that may fit better on your list of Priority Values:

- Accessibility

- Approachability

- Awareness

- Candor

- Intuition

- Listening

- Mindfulness

- Perception

- Professionalism

- Sincerity

7. The Value of Humility: The Extra Enchilada

How do you envision a humble person? Who is the humblest person you know? How would you describe that person without using the word humble?

Some of the greatest leaders I have known are incredibly humble. I have learned that as we more consistently focus on the value of humility, the better our lives and our relationships will be.

Author Chris Myers shared this truth in an article for *Forbes* titled "Why Humility Is So Important in Life, Leadership and Business." "No one likes dealing with egomaniacs," he wrote. "There are few things as off-putting as people who view themselves as being better than others or above the rules."[53]

---

53 Chris Myers, "Why Humility Is So Important in Life, Leadership and Business," Forbes, March 6, 2017, https://www.forbes.com/sites/chrismyers/2017/03/06/why-humility-is-so-important-in-life-leadership-and-business/2/#1830e0fa1732.

Myers recounts something his father taught him that encouraged him to remain humble even after he found success in his career. "Everybody falls down at some point," his father said. "Stay humble so that the people around you want to help you up, not knock you back down."[54]

It was humbling for me to go from being a prominent basketball player—where people usually looked up to me and sought my autograph—to a software salesman where people often looked down on me as I visited them in their stores. They were often too busy to take time to listen to me. Looking back, this difficult transition from stardom to salesman helped me to gain a new perspective on the value of humility.

The Arcade

Sometimes we are forced to be humble, sometimes we choose to be humble. I decided to buy an arcade in a pizza restaurant. The first time I had to set up a token machine, I couldn't make it work, so I called the manufacturer.

The call did not go well. Within minutes, the manufacturer was so upset with me that he raised his voice. I tried all the things he told me to do, but the machine would not work the way he thought it should.

> "Beware of false knowledge; it is more dangerous than ignorance."
>
> – George Bernard Shaw, *Man and Superman.*

I was lost. This was a completely new world for me. I felt incompetent. I had no idea a simple machine could be so complicated. I turned to

---

54 Myers, "Why Humility Is So Important in Life, Leadership and Business."

someone who was more patient with me—my fix-it-all son-in-law—and we were able to resolve the issue.

This was a learning and growing process. We all try to forget the times we felt small and insignificant and choose to remember times and the people who helped and built us up. If we stay humble, people are inclined to encourage and lift us, rather than cheer when we are down.

One definition of humility is accepting that you are not better than others just because you have more experience. When I realize I'm interacting with someone who is less experienced than I am, I make an extra effort to be kind. I remember what it is like to be on the other side of things.

Mexican Food for Lunch

Humility doesn't often come easy for athletes. When the coaches at a high school basketball camp announced they were taking two star recruits and me to lunch, I was not very humble about it. I was excited to be aggressively recruited by major college coaches. I felt special. I felt like a big shot.

Our complimentary lunch was delicious and we ate a lot of Mexican food, enjoying every bite. I ate one too many enchiladas. We were all stuffed when we left the restaurant.

That afternoon we were slated to play in a three-on-three tournament. Sadly, our team was beaten by three humble kids who had been careful not to eat too much at their cafeteria lunch. They were ready to compete and badly wanted to win while we struggled to move. We were then placed in the consolation bracket, and even with a half-hearted effort, we won the next game. My high school coach, Jim Spencer, who was helping at the camp and witnessed the game, was not impressed by my post-lunch efforts. He chastised me for going through the motions and not really trying.

"Every opponent," he said, "deserves your best effort and your respect." He taught me a lesson in humility I'll never forget.

My Wise Attorney

As a new real estate investor, I had the opportunity to buy a 39-unit apartment complex near a major university. I was excited about the property. Its close proximity to the university ensured high demand. Students wanted to live at that location, especially those who liked to wake up about five minutes before class and dash out the door.

I toured the property and began negotiating with the owner. We agreed on a price I thought was too high, but I was reluctant to push back because I wanted the property.

After running the numbers through my analyzer spreadsheet, I realized I would only get a 3 percent return on my invested capital. I took the proposal to my attorney, Scott Loveless. He was not excited, which surprised me.

"Tell me about the building," he said.

"It's in great shape," I responded. "One corner of the foundation settled and sunk several inches, but it was repaired. It has an old boiler system, but I think it is working well. The structure is built of cinder blocks, and I am confident I can get a 3 percent return on the investment."

After I described this "diamond in the rough," Scott looked at me and asked, "Devin, why do you want to do this? The foundation has had problems, the boiler system is old, and you're going to get a 3 percent cash-on-cash return. Why do you want to do this?"

A little defensive, I said, "Well, it's in a great location and that's the key to a successful investment?"

Scott asked me to complete a list of due diligence items on the property and find out more information before buying the building.

Sighing, I snatched the list from him. In my arrogance I thought to myself, "He's an attorney. He just doesn't understand this opportunity."

Grumbling through the process, I did my homework, checked everything off his list, and I was excited to buy the property.

> In the mid-1980s researchers at Cleveland State University made a startling discovery.
>
> They conducted an experiment by creating two fictitious job candidates, David and John. The candidates had identical résumés and letters of reference. The only difference was that John's letter included the sentence, "Sometimes, John can be difficult to get along with." They showed the résumés to a number of personnel directors. Which candidate did the personnel directors overwhelmingly prefer? Difficult to get along with, John.
>
> The researchers concluded the criticism of John made praise of John more believable. Admitting John's wart actually helped sell John. Admitting flaws gives you more credibility.
>
> —Harry Beckwith, *Selling the Invisible*

Beneath the excitement though, a little thought nagged at me. Scott was right. The financials did not show a pretty picture. The investment made sense because of the location, but numbers-wise, it was a mistake, and I knew it. Before meeting with my attorney again, I manipulated the numbers so they looked better to both of us.

He was not fooled. After studying all of the information, he looked at me, puzzled by my enthusiasm.

"These numbers are not very attractive," he said. "Why are you willing to buy when the price is so high?"

I justified the price and told him I was sure it would work.

"Devin, you need to think about this one," he said, then adding, "You don't have to do this deal. There are other deals out there that are better than this one."

I rationalized away all my concerns. I shielded myself from reality and gave in to the excitement. I left his office, frustrated, and absolutely convinced that he just did not understand the opportunity in front of me.

I had to decide. I could go against the advice of my trusted friend and counselor and move forward with the purchase. Or I could acknowledge I had a lot to learn and wait patiently for a better real estate opportunity to become available.

I took a few days to think and humble myself. "Maybe Scott does get it," I thought. "Maybe he does understand. Maybe I'm the one in the wrong. Maybe there are better deals out there." I was impatient and frustrated, disappointed there was nothing currently available. I had money I wanted to invest. Logically, I knew other properties would come up for sale, but it was hard to walk away, which I soon did.

A few months later a superior property came on the market. I was able to buy it because I was not saddled with an old apartment complex with a 3 percent return and a host of maintenance headaches.

I'm grateful to my dear friend Scott, one of the wisest people I have interacted with. He left this world in 2012, and I miss him.

Be Coachable

Watching Charles Barkley on television today, you may not believe me when I assure you he was a humble, coachable man during his college years. Charles had a Hall of Fame NBA career and is now a very successful commentator.

I had the opportunity to play on the same team with Charles Barkley and witnessed his skills as a basketball player firsthand. Today, he is well-known for his unapologetic banter. I remember Charles fondly for the time he did not say a word.

During one particular game, Barkley made a rare mistake. Rare, but still damaging. The coach pulled him out and Barkley sat near me on the bench. Stomping over, the coach did not hold back as he yelled at Barkley for the mistake, then yelled some more. Barkley took it. He did not say a word. When the coach put him back in the game, Charles made the necessary adjustments and played well. That's the value of humility, of being coachable.

He responded well to the criticism, and I wanted to be like that. When we are chastised, we can choose our response. We can become angry, bitter, shout back and make the situation a power struggle, destroying trust and relationships. Or we can take it, learn from it, make the necessary adjustments and hopefully avoid similar conversations with the coach in the future. That is not easy to do in the heat of the moment.

Don't Blame Others

Sadly, our society, from top to bottom, seems to be heading in a direction where we are quick to place blame on anyone but ourselves. Confident leaders who aren't looking for someone to blame are becoming hard to find today.

On this point, we could learn a lot from one of our past US presidents. President John F. Kennedy suffered an abysmal failure after the United States tried to invade Cuba and remove the communist government of Fidel Castro. The Bay of Pigs operation "became one of the greatest military fiascoes in American history."[55]

Kennedy addressed the failure. He acknowledged that the mission was a complete failure. He did not blame anyone for what occurred. He did not try to spin the situation in his favor. Most importantly, he humbly assumed complete responsibility.

The Benefit of the Doubt

We all make mistakes. Sometimes those mistakes are visible to thousands, as was the case with President Kennedy, and sometimes we are the only witness. How do we treat those who make mistakes? Do we quickly condemn them, or do we wait for more information? Sadly, most of us err on the side of quick condemnation. I like the old adage, "There are two sides to every pancake." A humble person always gives the benefit of the doubt and seeks to understand the "other side of the pancake."

I am reminded of the story, originally derived from a Welsh folk tale,[56] of the man in the cabin in the forest who is caring for a baby. He needs to leave the cabin for a time and trusts the care of the baby to his loyal dog. Upon his return, the man enters the cabin and is terrified to find the dog covered in blood. He quickly jumps to the conclusion that the dog has mauled and killed the baby during his absence. In a rage, he pulls out his knife and kills the dog. Shortly thereafter, he hears the cry of the baby. He goes to the room of the baby and beside the crib he

---

55 Christopher Klein, "Why the Bay of Pigs Invasion Went So Wrong," History, May 6, 2019, https://www.history.com/news/bay-of-pigs-mistakes-cuba-jfk-castro.

56 Ben Johnson, "The Legend of Gelert the Dog," Historic UK, https://www.historic-uk.com/HistoryUK/HistoryofWales/The-legend-of-brave-Gelert/.

finds the bloodied corpse of a wolf. The man drops to his knees as he realizes he has killed his courageous and loyal dog who had protected the baby from the predator wolf.

At times, in our pride and haste, we jump to unnecessary and unwise conclusions. By seeking delta through the value of humility, we more readily give the benefit of the doubt to those whom we may have condemned in the past or to whom we may be tempted to hastily judge in the future.

True Humility

I have always been impressed by these words spoken by Jesus Christ: "For I came down from heaven, not to do mine own will, but the will of him that sent me."[57]

It seems to me that the natural man would think a bit differently and want to do things his own way and not be subjected to the guidelines and principles of someone else. Jesus Christ, in all humility, embraced the opportunity to do the will of His Father.

Humility Grade

What is your value of humility grade? It seems counterintuitive to grade your humility, but it can be done. The following ideas might help you improve your humility delta and add value to you and your organization.

Humility Tools

Consider the following suggestions as ways to create the humility delta you would like to achieve. Please add additional tools that may not be included here.

1. Always show respect for people, property, and possessions.

---

57 "John 6:38," KJV, https://www.kingjamesbibleonline.org/John-6-38/.

2. Be open to advice from those closest to you—even if you feel it might be questionable.

3. Get to know the people around you, even if you have a fancier title and a higher pay grade.

4. Be coachable. Be teachable.

5. Be patient with yourself and others.

6. Take responsibility when things go wrong. Share the praise when things go right.

7. And going back to author Chris Myers, just be kind. "Always treat people the way you want to be treated," he writes. "I know it might sound simplistic and trite to some, but you can never go wrong with following the Golden Rule."[58]

The V Effect of humility ripples within our sight and beyond.

Below are 10 more values from Appendix 1 that align with the value of humility:

- Empathy
- Accomplishment
- Calmness
- Character
- Elegance
- Encouragement
- Fairness
- Learning
- Prudence

---

58 Myers, "Why Humility Is So Important in Life, Leadership and Business."

- Restraint
- Understanding

8. The Value of Initiative: Five Years to Live

Initiative is the last value on my current Priority Values list. It's the key to making the suggestions I've offered throughout this book meaningful in your life. Without the value of initiative, no action is taken. With the value of initiative, there are few limits on what you can achieve.

20,000 Shots

At the end of my freshman year at BYU, the basketball team met together before the summer break. The coaches challenged us to work hard over the summer and prepare for the following season. They asked each team member to make 20,000 shots, fill out progress reports, work on skill development, weightlifting, and conditioning. What? Make 20,000 shots? That would take so much time and effort to *make* 20,000 baskets. From the looks on my teammates' faces, not everyone was on board. We were to report back in the fall with our progress charts.

Summer passed, and we came back to school, and met together to report our progress at our first team meeting prior to the start of a new season.

Only about half of us had our progress charts. The others, for one reason or another, had lost theirs, although they reported they had shot a lot of shots and made good progress during the summer. A few players, including me, recorded their work and had documented 20,000 shots made. My sisters Kathryn and Marinda did a lot of rebounding for me that summer.

Our coach asked Mike Maxwell how many shots he had made over the summer. Mike said softly, "100,000." Everybody was stunned, but we all knew if Mike said he made 100,000 shots, he had. Mike Maxwell would never lie. He was one of the greatest shooters any of us had ever played with. Mike had been an All-American in high school and was on his way to becoming an All-American in college. Unfortunately, he suffered a serious knee injury that hindered his playing during the rest of his college career.

> "If you're trying to achieve, there will be roadblocks. I've had them; everybody has had them. But obstacles don't have to stop you. If you run into a wall, don't turn around and give up. Figure out how to climb it, go through it, or work around it."
>
> – Michael Jordan, *I Can't Accept Not Trying*

Mike had grown up playing basketball. His dad was his high school coach and instilled in Mike the desire to be a great basketball player. He helped Mike develop a love of the game and gym. Mike spent more hours working on his game than the rest of us.

Why was Mike so driven? He learned to coach himself. He was willing to do the small and simple things that make a powerful difference.

He magnified the value of initiative. He did not need anyone to push him. No one could push Mike harder than he pushed himself, and he sustained his effort over a long period of time.

The Flag Lot

In the professional world, it can be difficult at times to find Mike Maxwells—those people who do not need to be monitored all the time, are willing to take initiative, and supervise themselves to the next level.

I hired a recent college graduate named Brian Dabb. Brian understood the value of initiative. He was a model employee who looked around, saw what needed to be done, and did it. He treated my company like it was his company. He felt pride in his work. He was thorough. He was diligent. He amazed me with his talent, intelligence, and ingenuity. My decision to hire Brian turned out to be a very good one.

His primary job at the beginning of our relationship was to respond to maintenance requests like leaky faucets and broken electrical outlets. After making repairs, he always asked himself, "What can I do next? How can I make the property better?"

At one time I bought a half-acre lot with a nice house on it. A few years later, I was ready to sell the property. Brian advised against it. "Don't sell the entire lot and the house," he said. "You can subdivide the lot into two lots, sell off the house with the lot it sits on, and keep the new subdivided lot."

"I can't do that," I said.

"Sure, you can," Brian affirmed. "You just create a flag lot; there's enough ground to do that."

I smiled and asked Brian to pursue that option and get back to me.

He put together a plan and worked with the city and met all the ordinance requirements. Due to Brian's initiative and knowledge, a significant quantitative value delta was added to our business and I still own that flag lot. His vision became a reality and I am grateful— so grateful that I'm thinking about building my retirement home on the land Brian carved out to help our business years ago.

Breast Cancer

In 2013, Melanie Day was pregnant with her third child when she was diagnosed with breast cancer.

I had the privilege of talking with her in 2018 and this is part of what she told me:

> I withstood six rounds of AC (Adriamyacin Cytoxan) chemotherapy and a mastectomy while pregnant. Somehow my baby remained healthy throughout it all and was born without any complications.
>
> After the birth of our miracle baby, I endured radiation and Taxol chemotherapy. I have been on a year of Herceptin, ongoing hormone therapy and have had multiple surgeries for breast reconstruction. I was cancer free for one year, until the cancer returned in October of 2015. I have been given two to five years to live.

I was profoundly touched by Melanie's story. She has shared her inspiration in various interviews to live life to the fullest from the perspective of a cancer victim.[59]

---

59 Danielle Davis, "Motivating Mother—Melanie Pearson Day," Today's the Best Day, March 13, 2014, https://www.todaysthebestday.com/motivating-mother-melanie-day/; Madeline Buhman, "Staring Death in the Face," BYU Alumni, May 25, 2017, https://alumni.byu.edu/cougs-you-should-know/staring-death-face.

If you were to become terminally ill, would you take the initiative to forget yourself and help others? If you are perfectly healthy and whole, do you have the initiative to look around, help others, and fully live your life in harmony with your values? It is not necessary to run faster than you have strength but putting aside your fears and showing love to others can be the best medicine to overcome many of life's struggles.

Much to my delight, Melanie Day in 2019 became an assistant basketball coach for the Brigham Young University women's team. She has had clear cancer scans for the last three years. I often wonder how much her mental outlook plays in her current health condition. Keep it going, Melanie!

Finding Your Motivation

I am amazed by young kids who set their sights on a goal, and no matter what never take their eyes off it. They work hard to achieve dreams that are just that—dreams. When Tim Tebow was 11 years old, he was doing 400 push-ups and 400 sit-ups a day. Tim's father did not allow him to lift weights until he reached puberty, so Tebow did what he thought would build his strength.

> "People who are unable to motivate themselves must be content with mediocrity, no matter how impressive their other talents."
>
> – Attributed to Andrew Carnegie

He was motivated by the workout habits of the legendary Herschel Walker. When Walker was 12, he did 300 push-ups and 300 sit-ups a day. Tebow worked hard, added value to himself by becoming stronger mentally and physically, and committed to do even better.[60]

Steve and Lee

Every Fourth of July the Freedom Festival in Provo, Utah, hosts a 10K run and I participate. Years ago, while preparing for the race, I took note of the fact that Steve Young and Lee Johnson were also running.

Steve and Lee were graduates of BYU, and both had successful careers in professional football. Steve was a Hall of Fame quarterback and Lee was a legendary punter. We knew and supported each other in college but later went our separate ways.

The morning of the race, I laced up my high-top basketball shoes and got myself mentally ready to beat those NFL players. Wearing basketball shoes was not the best choice for a 10K, but I wanted to make a point. I am a basketball player and I was going to outrun these football players in less-than-ideal footwear.

We saw each other along the course. They teased me about my big, bulky basketball shoes, but I wasn't offended because my shoes and I left them in my wake early in the race. Right at the finish line, Lee and Steve appeared, and they both beat me.

The next year, I left my basketball shoes in the closet. I needed every advantage to beat my friends. These amazing athletes didn't care who came in first, but I did. While they were out for a recreational jog, I wanted to make sure I crossed the finish line before them.

They became my motivation to stay in shape. That simple competition was all I needed to prepare better, work harder, and run faster.

---

60 Mike Klis, "'Will to Win:' Excerpts from The Denver Post's Chronicle of Tim Tebow and the 2011 Broncos," The Denver Post, January 21, 2012, https://www.denverpost.com/2012/01/21/will-to-win-excerpts-from-the-denver-posts-chronicle-of-tim-tebow-and-the-2011-broncos-2/.

Rejection

Another failure proved to be a blessing to me. Nothing prepared me better to embrace the value of initiative than playing basketball; not because I was naturally good at the sport, but because one day I was *not* good enough.

When I was in third grade I excelled in math and spelling. Since I was ahead of my peers in these two subjects and bored with coloring flags of the world as a time-filling activity, I was given the opportunity to go to the fourth grade class for these two subjects. I settled in nicely in the fourth grade class. Eventually my parents, teachers, and principal decided to advance me to the fourth grade. In the middle of my third grade year, I suddenly became a fourth grader.

After a few days of jumping rope at recess with my new fourth grade friends, I wanted a new challenge. I noticed some fifth graders shooting baskets during recess. That looked fun. I learned they played basketball together after school, so I invited myself to play.

Eleven boys showed up. Two captains were appointed, and player by player, teams were chosen. Technically, I was in the fourth grade, but physically I was a third grader and smaller than the older boys. One spot remained to be filled. I was one of two boys left to be picked. I stood straight and tall, but the other guy was chosen and I was left to sit on the sidelines. There was no room for an 11th player, me. I could stay and watch or go home.

I felt rejected and began to cry. Then I got angry and decided I never wanted to be left out of a game again, and small as I was, I took the initiative and went to work. That critical step as a young boy was the beginning of my athletic delta. Be willing to take the initiative step no matter how old you are.

> "It will never rain roses: when we want to have more roses, we must plant more trees."
>
> – George Eliot, "The Spanish Gypsy," 1868

I practiced at home and my dad and older brother helped me. My family moved a few times, but no matter where we lived, Dad made sure there was a basketball hoop and a court to play on in the backyard. I played with friends, I played with family, and I played with strangers.

As a seventh grader, I tried out for the seventh and eighth grade combined team in Louisville, Kentucky, and made the team. I became a Seneca Redskin, thrilled to wear the red and gold.

The next year, I pushed myself and tried out for the ninth grade team and became the only eighth grader to make the team. I was initially excited, but I was miserable after the first week. The coach was demanding and stretched us all to our limits. While it wasn't much fun, he turned out to be the perfect coach for me at that stage of life. He paid attention to details and pushed me, and I learned to push myself and maintain that drive, positively affecting many aspects of my teenage years and beyond.

Growth Mindset

I have a grandson named Rockwell Devin Bennett, who I call Rock Devin. When he was six years old, he took me aside to talk. He was my teacher; I was his pupil.

His schoolteacher, Miss Bothaina, had studied the teachings of Dr. Carol Dweck,[61] which she shared with Rock Devin, and he with me.

---

61 Carol S. Dweck, Mindset: The New Psychology of Success (New York: Ballantine Books, 2006).

He asked: "Grandpa, do you know the difference between a *fixed mindset* and a *growth mindset*?" I shook my head and asked him to tell me the answer.

"First," Rock Devin said, "I'm going to talk about growth. Growth mindsets are when you say, 'I'm going to keep working at this, I'm going to keep trying at this. I can't give up.' That's called a growth mindset.

"And then you've got fixed, which is 'I give up. I'm not going to do this anymore. It's way too hard.' That's fixed.

"So, you always want to try growth. Maybe it's okay to sometimes have fixed but try to have growth."

That was all he said. I'll never forget this powerful message from my six-year-old grandson. Growth mindsets and the value of initiative go hand in glove.

Initiative Grade

How do you measure yourself with the value of initiative? What grade have you given yourself? The following initiative tools are designed to help you improve your initiative grade and create delta for your organization and you.

Initiative Tools

I was 39 years old the day I retired. I relaxed and slept more. I exercised. I read a little and ate a lot. It was *awful*. My test-run with retirement was a complete failure after a few days.

> "The superior man is modest in his speech, but exceeds in his actions."
>
> – Confucius, *The Analects*

I wanted to find the next investment opportunity. It was out there, waiting for me. I could feel it. I was programmed to make things happen.

It reminded me of when we looked for pick-up basketball games at the park. I refused to sit on the sidelines and wanted to get in the game. I wanted the challenge.

When will I stop working? I don't know. As long as the drive is there, I'll be looking for the next solid investment because I enjoy creating financial delta and adding value to my company.

I know that initiative is vital, particularly when venturing out on your own. What is your plan to take more initiative in your pursuits?

Here are some ideas to consider:

1. **Get to Work.** If something is to be done, you will do it. When you believe in yourself and get to work, you begin your journey to success. Sometimes, we get caught trying to decide between good options and are unable to choose. Don't allow yourself to become stagnant.

   When faced with two good choices, do your homework as best you can, then make your decision. Your subsequent efforts will be the main determining factor if it was the right decision.

2. **Be Willing to Take Risks.** Some people are more comfortable clocking in at 8 a.m. and clocking back out in the evening and being done with it. Owning a business is more of a risk. If you are a business owner, you can learn to enjoy taking on responsibility and accountability. Become comfortable showing initiative. Don't get overwhelmed when someone calls you late at night to tell you a car has crashed into one of your buildings.

That happened to me—twice. Enjoy the risk and autonomy and stress of not getting a predictable paycheck.

3. **Show Courage.** If you go down the path of an entrepreneur, no one outside your family will pay much attention to you. Nobody is keeping you in line and telling you what to do. Your success or failure is all on your shoulders. You have to fight and work and make things happen. It takes courage to take the leap and step into the unknown.

4. **Be Flexible Enough to Try, Try Again.** Every successful manager, executive, and administrator is prepared to analyze procedures to discover what is working and what is not. Businesses and other organizations often fail because leaders refuse to adjust or pivot. Refusing to be accountable, and pointing fingers at others, are bad habits that are becoming prevalent in our society. The problem with making excuses for our failures is that most of the time it works. If it works once, then it works twice. If you want to embrace the value of initiative, you must ultimately look back at yourself and your practices when things go wrong.

One of my favorite biblical verses applies here: "Be ye doers of the word, not hearers only, deceiving your own selves."[62]

Take the initiative. Make it happen. You can do it!

If the value of initiative didn't make your list of Priority Values, you might consider including one of the following values from Appendix 1:

- Ambition

- Assertiveness

- Boldness

---

62 "James 1:22," KJV, https://www.kingjamesbibleonline.org/James-1-22/.

- Drive

- Growth

- Improvement

- Motivation

- Persistence

- Resolve

- Toughness

The Values Delta: Take Small and Simple Steps

I believe that great results begin with small and simple steps. Mark my words: Your small and simple steps to create delta by focusing on your values, and how they impact the people and things that matter most to you, will be well-rewarded.

Give my system a try. There is no downside. If you haven't already, fill out The Values Delta Report Card for yourself and your organization. Test the process for a month or two. If you see a positive delta in yourself or those close to you, try it for another month or two. Watch your VPA go up. I hope it becomes a never-ending process of seeking delta with the people and things that enrich your life. You can do it!

Do you remember my two fictional friends from Part One, Michelle and Rick? Things worked out well for them, but they aren't real. *You* are. You and your organization are real with real challenges. May this book help you feel more hope and confidence in traveling the road ahead!

This book is the beginning of an outreach to encourage people to lift themselves and others to a better place by systematically reemphasizing their values and what is truly important to them. I have shared my Priority Values with you as a starting point and I plan to keep sharing ideas and stories (gathered from you) about other values that bring joy and purpose and meaning to our lives.

I hope when someone asks you what your secret to a happy and successful life is, you might say something like, "I strive to create positive delta for those people and things that matter most to me." You could then add, "I do it by focusing on my values in both my personal and professional life."

Stay In Touch

You've read many of my stories, and now I look forward to reading your stories of how you have focused on your values and the difference it has made. Also, share what you are learning and how you are growing with a family member, a trusted friend, a coworker, a faith leader, or someone who will encourage you in your quest to become your best self.

I hope you will feel comfortable sharing your experiences with me, so I can share them with others. Please visit my website at thevaluesdelta.com to contact me and get more information.

Devin Durrant

Acknowledgments

I have strong feelings about the importance of the values each of us embrace over the course of our lives. These feelings are a result of interacting with a wide range of people who have demonstrated to me the power of living by one's moral values. I offer my thanks to those people who have impacted my life in this way. Your names would fill many pages. Forgive me for not naming each of you here. Your names are written on my heart.

Many people have contributed to the writing and editing of this book. Others have helped by reading early versions of this book and offering helpful feedback.

I am immensely grateful to my wife, Julie, for her willingness to read and reread my manuscript. She has been my main motivation to move this book forward. Without her loving nudges this project would forever be "in the development stages."

I am also grateful to my six children and their spouses for their encouragement: Emily and Bryson, Laura and Spencer, Heather and

Danaan, Ryan and Valerie, Joseph and Rachel, and my youngest child, Deanna. I thank my parents and siblings for their values-based examples and help with the formulation of the ideas shared in this book: Father George and Mother Marilyn, Susan, Matthew, Kathryn, Marinda, Dwight, Warren, Sarah, and Mark.

I also wish to thank several dear friends and colleagues for their editing work, research, and thoughtful and wise suggestions: Tad Callister, Brian Ashton, Emily Furner, Lon Henderson, Phil Hoopes, Sr., Jan Heriford, Susan Woods, Edward Reid, Alicia Cunningham, David M. R. Covey, Brian Hansbrow, Chad Lewis, Stephen M.R. Covey, Pete Peterson, Andrew Hooge, Clive Winn, Emily Spackman and her stellar students at Brigham Young University, and Dr. David Bennett and his terrific team.

Family and Friends—two of my favorite words.

Author's Note

Thank you for reading *The Values Delta: A Small and Simple Way to Make a Positive Difference in Your Personal and Professional Life*. All profits from sales of *The Values Delta* will be donated to groups focused on lifting and inspiring others by highlighting their values and how those values make a positive difference in their lives and in their organizations. To learn more, visit thevaluesdelta.com.

APPENDIX 1: VALUES LIST

Acceptance	Competitiveness	Encouragement	Honor
Accessibility	Composure	Endurance	Hope
Accomplishment	Confidence	Energy	Hospitality
Accountability	Connection	Engagement	Humility
Accuracy	Consistency	Enjoyment	Humor
Achievement	Contentment	Entertainment	Hygiene
Adaptability	Contribution	Enthusiasm	Imagination
Adventure	Conviction	Equality	Impact
Affection	Cooperation	Ethics	Impartiality
Agility	Coordination	Excellence	Improvement
Ambition	Cordiality	Excitement	Independence
Amusement	Courage	Exuberance	Individuality
Anticipation	Courtesy	Experience	Industry
Appreciation	Craftsmanship	Expertise	Initiative
Approachability	Creativity	Exploration	Innovation
Assertiveness	Credibility	Fairness	Insight
Attentiveness	Curiosity	Faithfulness	Inspiration
Awareness	Daring	Fashion	Integrity
Balance	Decency	Fidelity	Intelligence
Beauty	Decisiveness	Fierceness	Intensity
Belonging	Dedication	Fitness	Intuition
Boldness	Delight	Flair	Invention
Bravery	Dependability	Flexibility	Joy
Brilliance	Depth	Focus	Justice
Calmness	Determination	Foresight	Kindness
Candor	Devotion	Freedom	Knowledge
Capability	Dignity	Friendship	Leadership
Carefulness	Diligence	Frugality	Learning
Caring	Discipline	Fun	Liberty
Change	Discovery	Generosity	Listening
Character	Discretion	Giving	Logic
Charity	Diversity	Goodness	Love
Cheerfulness	Drive	Gratitude	Loyalty
Cleanliness	Duty	Growth	Mastery
Collaboration	Eagerness	Guidance	Maturity
Comfort	Education	Happiness	Meekness
Commitment	Effectiveness	Harmony	Meticulousness
Common Sense	Efficiency	Health	Mindfulness
Communication	Elegance	Helpfulness	Moderation
Compassion	Empathy	Holiness	Modesty
Competency	Empowerment	Honesty	Motivation

APPENDIX 1: VALUES LIST

Mystery	Preservation	Sacrifice	Temperance
Neatness	Privacy	Safety	Thankfulness
Obedience	Proactivity	Satisfaction	Thoroughness
Openness	Productivity	Security	Thoughtfulness
Optimism	Professionalism	Selflessness	Timeliness
Order	Profitability	Sensitivity	Tolerance
Organization	Progress	Serenity	Toughness
Originality	Prosperity	Service	Tranquility
Passion	Prudence	Sharing	Transparency
Patience	Punctuality	Simplicity	Trust
Patriotism	Purity	Sincerity	Truth
Peace	Quality	Skillfulness	Understanding
Perception	Reason	Solitude	Uniqueness
Perfection	Recognition	Speed	Unity
Performance	Recreation	Spirituality	Usefulness
Perseverance	Reflection	Spontaneity	Valor
Persistence	Relationships	Stability	Variety
Philanthropy	Relaxation	Status	Vigor
Playfulness	Reliability	Stewardship	Virtue
Pleasantness	Resilience	Strength	Vision
Poise	Resolve	Structure	Vitality
Polish	Resourcefulness	Success	Warmth
Positivity	Respect	Support	Watchfulness
Potential	Responsibility	Surprise	Welcoming
Power	Responsiveness	Sustainability	Winning
Pragmatism	Restraint	Sympathy	Wisdom
Precision	Results	Synergy	Work
Preparation	Reverence	Talent	

APPENDIX 2: THE VALUES DELTA REPORT CARD
8-Week Plan (Individual)

Section 1 / Section 2

My Priority Values I would describe myself as a person of...	Grades (Begin) 1.0-4.0	Grades (End) 1.0-4.0	Things I Value My life would be much less meaningful without...
1.			My name: 1.
2.			2.
3.			3.
4.			4.
5.			5.
6.			6.
7.			7.
8.			8.
Total =			My Values
My VPA (Total/__) =			Delta =

Section 3

My Priority Value Focus? Choose one value from the My Priority Values list for each of the eight weeks below.		One Thing I Value? Choose one thing on the Things I Value list for each of the eight weeks below. Duplicate use is okay.	Focus Actions? A-Quote B-Picture C-Read/Listen D-Discuss E-Activity	

My Focus Value...	Week	Dates	I Value...	A-E	Y/N
	1				
	2				
	3				
	4				
	5				
	6				
	7				
	8				

APPENDIX 3: THE VALUES DELTA REPORT CARD
8-Week Plan (Organization)

Section 1 / Section 2

Our Priority Values We would describe ourselves as an organization of...	Grades (Begin) 1.0-4.0	Grades (End) 1.0-4.0	Things We Value Our organization would be much less meaningful without...
1.			Our name: 1.
2.			2.
3.			3.
4.			4.
5.			5.
6.			6.
7.			7.
8.			8.
Total =			Our Values
Our VPA (Total/__) =			Delta =

Section 3

Our Priority Value Focus? Choose one value from the Our Priority Values list for each of the eight weeks below.	THE VALUES DELTA	One Thing We Value? Choose one thing on the Things We Value list for each of the eight weeks below. Duplicate use is okay.	Focus Actions? A-Quote B-Picture C-Read/Listen D-Discuss E-Activity	

Our Focus Value...	Week	Dates	We Value...	A-E	Y/N
	1				
	2				
	3				
	4				
	5				
	6				
	7				
	8				

APPENDIX 4: THE VALUES DELTA REPORT CARD — MICHELLE
8-Week Plan (Individual)

Section 1 / Section 2

My Priority Values I would describe myself as a person of...	Grades (Begin) 1.0-4.0	Grades (End) 1.0-4.0	Things I Value My life would be much less meaningful without...
1. Thoughtfulness	3.0	3.5	**My name:** 1. Michelle
2. Caring	3.5	4.0	2. Children
3. Industriousness	2.5	3.0	3. Legal career
4. Creativity	3.5	3.75	4. Friends
5. Wisdom	3.0	3.25	5. Horse ranch
6. Generosity	2.5	3.0	6.
7.			7.
8.			8.
Total =	18.00	20.50	My Values
My VPA (Total/__) =	3.00	3.42	Delta = .42

Section 3

My Priority Value Focus? Choose one value from the My Priority Values list for each of the eight weeks below.		One Thing I Value? Choose one thing on the Things I Value list for each of the eight weeks below. Duplicate use is okay.	Focus Actions? A-Quote B-Picture C-Read/Listen D-Discuss E-Activity	

My Focus Value...	Week	Dates	I Value...	A-E	Y/N
Thoughtfulness	1	1-7	Michelle	A	Y
Caring	2	8-14	Children	B	N
Industriousness	3	15-21	Legal career	E	Y
Creativity	4	22-28	Legal career	D	Y
Wisdom	5	29-4	Horse ranch	C	Y
Generosity	6	5-11	Friends	A	Y
Creativity	7	12-18	Children	D	Y
Caring	8	19-25	Michelle	C	Y

APPENDIX 5: THE VALUES DELTA REPORT CARD— DBKC
8-Week Plan (Organization)

Section 1 / Section 2

Our Priority Values We would describe ourselves as an organization of…	Grades (Begin) 1.0-4.0	Grades (End) 1.0-4.0	Things We Value Our organization would be much less meaningful without…
1. Integrity	3.7	3.8	Our name: 1. DBKC Inc.
2. Customer service	3.0	3.5	2. Our employees
3. Respect	3.3	3.75	3. The families of our employees
4. Loyalty	3.0	3.25	4. Our customers
5. Vision	3.8	4.0	5. Our community relationship
6. Discipline	2.8	3.0	6.
7. Charity	3.0	3.9	7.
8. Punctuality	2.6	3.0	8.
Total =	26.00	28.20	Our Values
Our VPA (Total/__) =	3.25	3.53	Delta = **.28**

Section 3

Our Priority Value Focus? Choose one value from the Our Priority Values list for each of the eight weeks below.		One Thing We Value? Choose one thing on the Things We Value list for each of the eight weeks below. Duplicate use is okay.	Focus Actions? A-Quote B-Picture C-Read/Listen D-Discuss E-Activity	

Our Focus Value…	Week	Dates	We Value…	A-E	Y/N
Integrity	1	1-7	Our employees	A	Y
Customer Service	2	8-14	DBKC, Inc.	B	N
Respect	3	15-21	Our customers	E	Y
Loyalty	4	22-28	The families of our employees	D	Y
Vision	5	29-4	DBKC, Inc.	C	Y
Discipline	6	5-11	Our customers	A	Y
Charity	7	12-18	Our community relationship	B	Y
Punctuality	8	19-25	Our employees	C	Y

Blank Individual Report Cards

INDIVIDUAL REPORT CARD
8-Week Plan (Individual)

Section 1

My Priority Values I would describe myself as a person of…	Grades (Begin) 1.0-4.0	Grades (End) 1.0-4.0
1.		
2.		
3.		
4.		
5.		
6.		
7.		
8.		
Total =		
My VPA (Total/__) =		

Section 2

Things I Value My life would be much less meaningful without…
My name: 1.
2.
3.
4.
5.
6.
7.
8.
My Values Delta =

Section 3

My Priority Value Focus?		One Thing I Value?	Focus Actions?	
Choose one value from the My Priority Values list for each of the eight weeks below.		Choose one thing on the Things I Value list for each of the eight weeks below. Duplicate use is okay.	A-Quote B-Picture C-Read/Listen D-Discuss E-Activity	

My Focus Value…	Week	Dates	I Value…	A-E	Y/N
	1				
	2				
	3				
	4				
	5				
	6				
	7				
	8				

INDIVIDUAL REPORT CARD
8-Week Plan (Individual)

Section 1   Section 2

My Priority Values I would describe myself as a person of…	Grades (Begin) 1.0-4.0	Grades (End) 1.0-4.0	Things I Value My life would be much less meaningful without…
1.			My name: 1.
2.			2.
3.			3.
4.			4.
5.			5.
6.			6.
7.			7.
8.			8.
Total =			**My Values Delta =**
My VPA (Total/__) =			

Section 3

My Priority Value Focus? Choose one value from the My Priority Values list for each of the eight weeks below.	**THE VALUES DELTA**	One Thing I Value? Choose one thing on the Things I Value list for each of the eight weeks below. Duplicate use is okay.	Focus Actions? A-Quote B-Picture C-Read/Listen D-Discuss E-Activity	
My Focus Value…	**Week**	**Dates**	**I Value…**	**A-E**	**Y/N**
	1				
	2				
	3				
	4				
	5				
	6				
	7				
	8				

Blank Organization Report Cards

ORGANIZATION REPORT CARD
8-Week Plan (Organization)

Section 1   Section 2

Our Priority Values We would describe ourselves as an organization of…	Grades (Begin) 1.0-4.0	Grades (End) 1.0-4.0	Things We Value Our organization would be much less meaningful without…
1.			Our name: 1.
2.			2.
3.			3.
4.			4.
5.			5.
6.			6.
7.			7.
8.			8.
Total =			**Our Values**
Our VPA (Total/__) =			**Delta =**

Section 3

| Our Priority Value Focus?
Choose one value from the Our Priority Values list for each of the eight weeks below. | THE VALUES DELTA | One Thing We Value?
Choose one thing on the Things We Value list for each of the eight weeks below. Duplicate use is okay. | Focus Actions?
A-Quote
B-Picture
C-Read/Listen
D-Discuss
E-Activity | |

Our Focus Value…	Week	Dates	We Value…	A-E	Y/N
	1				
	2				
	3				
	4				
	5				
	6				
	7				
	8				

ORGANIZATION REPORT CARD

8-Week Plan (Organization)

Section 1   Section 2

Our Priority Values We would describe ourselves as an organization of…	Grades (Begin) 1.0-4.0	Grades (End) 1.0-4.0	Things We Value Our organization would be much less meaningful without…
1.			Our name: 1.
2.			2.
3.			3.
4.			4.
5.			5.
6.			6.
7.			7.
8.			8.
Total =			Our Values
Our VPA (Total/__) =			Delta =

Section 3

Our Priority Value Focus? Choose one value from the Our Priority Values list for each of the eight weeks below.	THE VALUES DELTA	One Thing We Value? Choose one thing on the Things We Value list for each of the eight weeks below. Duplicate use is okay.	Focus Actions? A-Quote B-Picture C-Read/Listen D-Discuss E-Activity	

Our Focus Value…	Week	Dates	We Value…	A-E	Y/N
	1				
	2				
	3				
	4				
	5				
	6				
	7				
	8				

Manufactured by Amazon.ca
Bolton, ON

28270015R00114